THE STATE OF THEORY

Since the 1960s the object of literary studies has become increasingly problematic. Critical theory and cultural studies have combined to challenge traditional assumptions of what literature is, placing it on the same shifting territory as issues of gender, race and class. *The State of Theory* addresses the crucial pedagogical questions raised by the theoretical debate. Written by teachers who are also at the forefront of the development of critical theory, the contributions are challenging, diverse and celebratory.

Topics discussed include: race and gender in literary studies; the value of student 'theory guides'; the impact of theory on teaching practice, and the future for theory in English departments.

Richard Bradford is Lecturer in English at the University of Ulster. He is also the author of *A Linguistic History of English Poetry* (1993), part of the Routledge Language in Literary Studies series. His other titles include a guide to *Paradise Lost* (1992), *Silence and Sound: Theories of Poetics from the 18th Century* (1992) and *The Look of It: A Theory of Visual Form in English Poetry* (1993).

THE STATE OF THEORY

OF

THEORY

Edited by Richard Bradford

London and New York

First published 1993
by Routledge
11 New Fetter Lane, London EC4P 4EE

Simultaneously published in the USA and Canada
by Routledge
29 West 35th Street, New York, NY 10001

Typeset in Palatino by EXCEPT*detail* Ltd, Southport

Printed and bound in Great Britain by Clays Ltd,
St Ives plc

Printed on acid free paper

British Library Cataloguing in Publication Data
A catalogue record for this book is available from the
British Library

Library of Congress Cataloging in Publication Data
The State of Theory/edited by Richard Bradford.
p.   cm.
Includes bibliographical references and index.
1. Criticism. 2. Literature–Study and teaching (Higher)–
Great Britain.
PN81.S694 1993   93-14827
801′.95–dc20

ISBN 0-415-07323-5 (hbk)
ISBN 0-415-07324-3 (pbk)

CONTENTS

CONTENTS

CONTRIBUTORS

Richard Bradford (editor) is Lecturer in English at the University of Ulster.

Steven Connor is Reader in English at Birkbeck College, University of London.

Thomas Docherty is Professor of English at Trinity College, Dublin.

Antony Easthope is Professor of English, Manchester Metropolitan University.

Maggie Humm is Co-ordinator of Women's Studies at the University of East London.

K.M. Newton is Professor of English at the University of Dundee.

Patrick Parrinder is Professor of English at the University of Reading.

Tony Pinkney is Lecturer in English at Lancaster University.

Bernard Sharratt is Professor of English at the University of Kent at Canterbury.

Helen Taylor is Senior Lecturer in English at the University of Warwick.

PREFACE

The relationship between literature and the academic study of literature has never been a particularly happy one, and over the past three decades there have been rumours of a trial separation.

Since the end of the seventeenth century, novels, collections of short stories or poems, and performances of plays have been profitably sold to people who might want to entertain or divert themselves in those spare moments between their more pressing domestic or professional commitments. But, as we are regularly reminded, this lucrative monopoly of entertainment has for the past century had to endure competition from film, radio, television and other electronic media. So academics and students face a number of related arguments against the relevance and general usefulness of spending three (or now possibly two) years in the intensive study of English or comparative literature.

Knowing about narratology does not equip us to write saleable novels or screenplays or submit usable news copy. Nor is it of much use to those who do not re-enter the education system and who find themselves facing the non-literary requirements of the civil service, industry, marketing or self-employed pig farming. But it could be argued that civil servants, managers and pig farmers are united with refuse collectors, politicians and the unemployed in an addiction to reading stories, and that this addiction has sustained the profitability of the printed word against its electronic competitors. If many of us spend a significant part of our waking lives tracking through worlds and experiences created entirely by the linguistic resources of other people, should we not grant the study of this material a status roughly equivalent to the more practical imperatives of sociology, history, science and medicine? Perhaps we should, but even if such an argument can sustain English studies against the charges of non-vocationalism we still face the counter-arguments of elitism, prejudice and inaccessibility.

The title of literary or critical theory has been conferred upon a vast and usually divided academic growth industry that seeks to address these twin problems of the relevance and the practical benefits of studying literature in higher education. The contents of this collection will, I hope, reflect the breadth and, some might argue, the intrinsic instability of literary studies as an academic discipline. It is, in short, the state of theory. It does not claim to represent a particular or even a general hubris or objective. Matthew Arnold, Leavis, the New Critics, the structuralists and the poststructuralists should by now have demonstrated that the ideal of offering or justifying literary studies as a unified disciplinary function is as realisable as juggling with sand or a Green Party majority in the House of Commons. So, one might ask, what is the point of exposing, or even celebrating, a condition of unease and irreconcilable division? To answer this, I will move from the general to the particular.

A curious and paradoxical thread of unity runs through this collection, and it is most clearly identified in the recurrent references to T.S. Kuhn's theory of the shifting paradigm. The old paradigm of the objectives and assumptions of literary studies began to crumble, at least in Britain and the USA, at the beginning of the 1960s. The 1958 Indiana conference on linguistics and literary studies can be regarded as its curtain call. Roman Jakobson was its star and his paper on 'Linguistics and poetics' was subtitled, with brilliant if unintended irony, 'Closing statement'. Jakobson and his fellow participants disagreed on protocols and techniques, but they were enthusiastically united in their objective of defining the nature and function of the literary object. But the poststructuralists were waiting in the wings, and within a decade the notion of the literary text as distinguishable from practically everything else was no longer on the agenda. The new paradigm has arrived, but what is it? The energies and motivating forces of critical writing have shifted from a centripetal emphasis upon the constitution of the literary text to the centrifugal forces that sweep such artefacts into the diffuse and untidy cosmos of philosophy, gender studies, deconstruction, psychoanalysis, historicism and so on. Perhaps we should offer the new paradigm the prefix now carried by most of its constituent isms: we now inhabit the postparadigm. This collection reflects and embodies the postparadigmatic condition.

Pinkney tells us about the benefits of 'the Gothic' as a means of restoring some form of cool disorder to our postmodern condition, while Sharratt ponders the relationship between literature and the unmediated mainframe of electronic media, itself a very Gothic pairing. Parrinder warns of the danger of recycling theory as student-targeted textbooks and Connor distils a pure and unrecyclable draught of theory (still) at work. Newton is optimistic: the divisions of the past three decades can create a productive interface in teaching. Bradford agrees – or possibly not. Humm's chapter reflects the 'Eminence' of feminism and Black consciousness in the world of theory, and Easthope reminds the inhabitants of this global paradigm that 'a fairer Paradise is founded now'. For Docherty the difficulty of reading and writing literary theory is a token of its honesty: if the commentary is easier to understand than the poem then the commentator must be lying. And Taylor brings us back to the office and the classroom where we continue to celebrate the influence of feminism, popular culture, the new canon, while waiting anxiously for their arrival in the institution.

There are two ways of responding to this phenomenon of disciplinary pluralism. The first involves the perspective offered by the new sub-genre of the campus novel and its televised offshoots. In these, we encounter the amusing spectacle of intellectuals desperately trying to close their doors against the incursions of the real world and tripping over one another in the dark. And David Lodge was no doubt feeding upon the curious mixture of awe, respect and incomprehension still generated by the public image of the English 'English don' when he invented Robyn Penrose and Vic Wilcox, respectively the jargon-wielding theorist and the no-nonsense inhabitant of the real world. The question raised by this perspective is: why should anyone wish to become involved in an academic discipline which is directionless, divided and of only occasional entertainment value?

The answer involves a very different way of looking at this collection. The fact that English studies has become a dispersed, decentred phenomenon signals, paradoxically enough, the final unification of the discipline and its subject. Literature is and has always been a potentially chaotic synthesis of genres, disciplines, intentions, functions and effects. It is mimetic in the sense that it stands at the border between the anarchic and the formal, fabrication and truth, clarity and introspection, what might be and what is; and very few people would now deny that the human condition involves the constant slide between these uneasy partnerships. Anyone who still believes that the study of literature will guarantee access to high culture, standard morality, social responsibility or intellectual grandeur is either a politician or a fabricating opportunist – or, more likely, both. As each of the following contributors demonstrates, the postparadigmatic state of literary theory offers the student and the teacher the opportunity to explore the uncertain yet addictive relationship between literary writing and their own more immediate perceptions of enjoyment, diversion, class, history, gender, race . . . Literary critics and theorists might not be able to do or achieve anything in particular, but we involve just about everything.

Richard Bradford

1

CYBERTHEORY

Bernard Sharratt

OLD TRAINS OF THOUGHT

I have for a long time written satirical and political ballads and indeed performed them. Perhaps when I first began to write 'serious criticism', I never really saw a way of hooking that up with such more popular kinds of cultural activity. I would hope that, now, there is in my writing an attempt at a greater convergence between the two. And the same really applies to my novel: I was delighted when somebody said that what they liked about it was that, although it was an intellectual novel, it was not an academic novel . . . So, once again, to try to write, as they say, creatively but also intellectually would be a desirable stylistic and political goal. I am horrified by the dearth of ideas in contemporary English fiction, which I think has its roots in a certain ingrown English empiricism and commonsensicality, and I think that if there is to be a viable fiction of the left, as well as a theory, then it has to find ways of bringing creative and intellectual discourses together.

I was reading that final paragraph of Terry Eagleton's recent book, *The Significance of Theory*, while sitting in a train stalled at Nuneaton station. After I closed the book came the ritual of pondering.

That provincial Midland town of Nuneaton, outside my window, was where the young Marian Evans grew up, on her way to becoming the exemplarily mature George Eliot, author of *Middlemarch*, the quintessential novel of Leavis's great tradition, linchpin of EngLit courses for a generation. But she was also author of that major attempt at English intellectual political fiction, *Daniel Deronda*, selectively excised by the same F.R. Leavis, to be reconstituted and tamed as *Gwendolen Harleth*. As the train waited, I measured in memory the density of those great Victorian novels, their pace and length, the sense of journey embedded in their very structure, their linear narration and closure, their obvious relation to this very railway system which emerged with them and helped sustain them. Once, long ago, back in the early 1960s, in *The Long Revolution*, Raymond Williams had analysed the 1840s sales figures for novels sold on W.H. Smith's new railway kiosks as a way into explaining the 'structure of feeling' of a historical moment. I remembered the difficulty, and therefore the excitement, then, of advancing such analyses, entwining material history and critical analysis into a single argument, itself a step on the way to recognising the formal structuring of such fiction by its own modes of production, distribution and consumption. Familiar and now faded modes of theory. The cover of Terry Eagleton's very first book, endearingly entitled *The New Left Church*, included a picture of a railway station. Inside was a laconic analysis of how modern railways symbolised both connection and alienation, as a prelude to close 'practical criticism' of the structure of feeling in then-contemporary poetry. Very New Left. Very early Marx.

Marian Evans, en route to becoming George Eliot, moved from provincial backwater to national reputation via responsibility for a metropolitan journal, as effective editor of the *Westminster Review*. The journal as means of intervention and as defining a generation now has a long tradition. I still have a complete set of *Scrutiny* and a very long run of *New Left Review* (*NLR*). In 1968 *NLR*'s editor Perry Anderson 'placed' F.R. Leavis as neatly as he might have done it himself: a map of British culture centred on a displaced totalisation, literary criticism, itself to be displaced by the deliberate pantheon of New Left Books' continental translations throughout the 1970s. But Anderson's account left out both creative literature and the hard sciences: it was our 'concepts of man and society' that were crucial, and lacking. A severe dose of high theory was peremptorily prescribed. The piece was reprinted recently, in Anderson's *English Questions*, but even in its sequel, 'A culture in counterflow', Anderson's map still omits theatre, film and television as well as science. It also relegates to a single footnote the true theoretical successor to *NLR* itself, the *Screen* of the 1970s.

In my own university 'English' has remained largely uninfluenced by any explicit literary theory, but in the 1970s Kent set up degrees in Marxist studies and women's studies, a drama degree heavily influenced by Williams and a film studies course staffed by *Screen* editors. Then in the 1980s came a Lacaninspired MA in psychoanalytic studies, a Board of PostColonial Studies and a BA in a home-grown hybrid, 'communications and image studies'. Before getting on the train today I went to the railway bookstall, to buy not a novel or *NLR* but *Amiga Format* and *Byte*. Some years ago I stopped teaching literature and literary theory. Now I chair that multidisciplinary degree programme, 'communications and image studies', and spend much of my time initiating students into the multimedia possibilities of computers interfacing with video and sound. The long crawl of the intercity train gave me a chance to read the latest computer news and, for a while, *The Significance of Theory*.

(*Several years ago an EngLit colleague turned up for a meeting whitefaced. On inquiry his shock turned out to be caused not by news of cancer or redundancy but by an idle moment of calculation: he had just given his five hundredth supervision on* Middlemarch.)

MEMORIES OF THEORIES AND PRACTICES

So what now is the significance of theory? Part of the difficulty is knowing what theory is being contrasted with. The older formulations of a polarity of theory and practice tended to be dependent upon the theoretical position one adopted. If theory meant Marxism, the appropriate practice was to do with political revolution, with a definable agency, victim and purpose. If one's theoretical allegiance was primarily to psychoanalysis, the paradigmatic practice was ultimately the clinical. The chain of links between theory and practice might then stretch somewhat unconvincingly across several layers of other theory/practice couplings, negotiated step by step. At present, however, it seems that theory does not so readily, or guiltily, distinguish itself from practice, but rather assimilates practice into itself: the practice of writing being itself responsible, it can seem, for the construction of agencies and audiences, a self-generating autogestion. If, for Anderson, literary criticism was a substitute totalisation, at least the kind of totalisation involved was in continuity with George Eliot's: the ambition to make sense of a whole society, historically, sociologically and culturally. Marx could share that arena with Eliot and Marxists could self-persuasively align their functions as intellectuals with the places already prepared for the English 'cultural critic'. Williams had traced that lineage in his *Culture and Society* and located himself within it. But an old impasse had always been there.

(*At the launch meeting of the* May Day Manifesto, *in 1968, Williams, as editor, outlined its process of collaborative composition, recalling the long weekend of final paste-up: how the various single-issue analyses and expert local contributions, as they were placed next to each other on his table at home, had finally converged and intertwined, leading unmistakably towards political conclusion and stance, which in turn led, as the argument unfolded and spread along the table, to the inevitable question of agency and strategy . . . 'There,' Williams concluded enigmatically, 'the table ended.'*)

The once-dominant model (call it Model T) of the relation between theory and practice saw theory as a prerequisite and preliminary to practice; theory produced and informed analysis and without analysis no appropriate practice was possible. This model had its roots in the Marxist distinction between the underlying causal forces within a social formation (mapped as the economy) and the more dependent cultural components of that formation (base and superstructure). It was then the task of theoreticians (an aspect of all political activists) to understand those underlying forces, and this allegedly qualified them for correct strategic insight, equipping them with a surer basis for tactical intervention and influence. From *The Long Revolution* (*LR*) onwards one can trace in Williams's work the demolition of the foundations of this whole model. Yet at the same time the very format of his work re-enacted much the same basic model. In *LR* a theoretical first section was followed by several chapters of history, themselves succeeded by proposals and policies for the present. The implication of this formal arrangement was linear and hierarchical: establish the theory first, see the historical connections and then move to current practice. The very ambition of the historical chapters indicated one of the persistent problems of this model even within a formal

4

pedagogy: an unavoidably asymptotic curve on the historical material needing to be mastered. Any attempt to build, say, an interpretation of Jacobean drama on the foundations established by historical research rapidly embroiled one in the battles between sharply differing historians; either one's delayed and provisional contribution became merely that of an amateur onlooker waiting to see who had won, or one offered the analysis of the 'literature' also as one more contribution to the historical debate, a conflation of genres and disciplines that could end only with assimilation. A similar problem persisted for any theoretically informed politics: the endlessly procrastinated and asymptotic process of analytical 'rigour' that would finally pinpoint the revolutionary moment.

(*I once asked a student who had already done a highly specialised MA in Victorian literature, and was now taking a special period paper 1830–70, whether he would prefer to concentrate on one or two authors, say Tennyson or Clough. 'Does Tennyson come into that period?' he asked.*)

At a broad level, what succeeded this basic model did indeed collapse genre and discipline distinctions, as it did the relation between theory and practice. The initially influential version of this model (call it Model S) was Althusserian in tenor, and its most severe British manifestation signalled the appropriate shift in the very title of its inevitable journal: *Theoretical Practice*. Central to this still influential family of approaches and positions (theories) has been the notion that a social or discursive formation is at some level intradependently systemic, and that the linchpins of any such system are at root conceptual. In so far as the entire social order is theoretically characterised by one or two key organising principles, by a specific epistemic configuration, or by the spectacle or the simulacrum, any opponent is also recognised as a participant: the situationist is also a spectacle, Baudrillard is undeniably a simulacrum. This stance has one of its roots in Surrealism: the construction of a self-sustaining artefact enjoying a displaced and displacing relation to what one might otherwise have simplemindedly thought of as the real; the surreal offers not so much an alternative world as a disorienting recognition of the genuine oddity of the apparent world. The crucial practice is then a kind of theory, conceptual intervention, yet problematic, even pessimistic, since the very notion of agency tends to dissolve, while the issue of historical change and succession is rendered almost unthinkable. A long sequence of theoretical fashions, from Lévi-Strauss to Lacan, from Foucault to a resuscitated Debord, from Orientalism to Exterminism, can be grouped under this general rubric (Saussurean/structuralist/semiotic/ situationist, etc.).

Some of Terry Eagleton's later books bear a somewhat similar relation to this second strand of theoretical model as Williams's *Long Revolution* did to the first: a kind of textual counterpositioning. For example, *The Function of Criticism* is organised as a historical working through of the logic of 'criticism', from its inauguration in the public sphere of eighteenth-century journals and coffee houses to the present professionalised ghetto of conference papers and university departments. Yet in so far as the book's argument demonstrates that there is no longer a public sphere within which and through which criticism can have a political function and effect, the book thereby underwrites its own lack of function and becomes an artefact curiously held up only by its own creation of an audience, a kind of autotelic state of reproduction. Subsequently, and appropriately, *The Ideology of the Aesthetic* replays at a more overtly philosophical level the trajectory sketched more locally in Williams's *Culture and Society*, but both seem over-indebted to a historical moment of mediation that has now passed. Both Marxist and Conservative uses of aesthetics and culture derive, arguably, not so much from Romanticism or German Idealist theory but from a phase in mid-Victorian England when the crucial and pragmatic ideological function of 'culture' was to help compose a single hegemonic block by reconstituting a common class identity for the successors of the two contending classes of the long revolution of the eighteenth century. (*By this time my train was passing through Rugby: faint echoes of Tom Brown's miserable public school days, of Thomas Arnold and his sad sons.*) But as organised democratic demands successfully extended the formal franchise, that reliance on culture as hegemonising cement was transmuted. From being an inward constitutive of a new ruling class self-consciousness and sensibility, 'culture' was increasingly offered, in the mass newspapers of the nineteenth century and the mass media of the twentieth, as an external and so-called 'national heritage', dangled discriminatingly before an 'uncultured' subordinate class but with the promise of incorporation and assimilation.

The underlying move here was effectively to separate knowledge from power, to offer an unprecedented dramatising of society freely available to all citizens, manufacturing an imagined community across a national breakfast table or television tray, yet at the same time to restrict any actual engagement in political decision-making to an occasional intervention in the private election booth. Within this process the deeply identificatory effect of those literary devices of totalisation, linearity and closure became sufficiently generalised and incorporated into the popular generic forms of the new media as to make actual literature largely redundant, and as 'Literature' became marginalised, so did the critical function of debate around literature. Any radical still operating from within that inherited arena had to retrain as an expert combatant in general semiotic systems. Whereas Williams could, initially, speak from within a secure territorial base and a known community allegiance (not least as a historical novelist of an ambitiously totalising kind), Eagleton had the generationally later task of becoming an assault commando in a cultural no man's land, a cyberspace cowboy of the intellectual matrix, attacking the shifting theoretical ice of artificially intelligent ideological formations, assaulting the institutionally entrenched defence systems of capitalist academia, hacking into the secret spaces and inner recesses of ideological manufacture, exposing its trade secrets and advance sales strategies. It was invigorating but sometimes seemed like misplaced energy: dammit, why didn't he write about politics instead?

(*I once asked Eagleton why he wanted to write a book on Walter Benjamin. So that the* New York Review of Books *doesn't get there first, was the reply.*)

POSTBINARIES: FROM THE *SUN* TO SONY AND SUN

As literary criticism glided from theory to theory to metatheory, one response argued that the appropriate targets in this sophisticated war of position were not the Metaphysical poets and John Bayley, or even the metaphysics of presence, but nationalist myopia and Rupert Murdoch and, for example, the *Sun*'s advertising pages as the self-representation of capitalist commodity. Nevertheless, even a semiotic deconstruction of a

Chanel ad or a page three girl was hardly likely to undermine the grip of Saatchi and Saatchi, let alone NATO, and, as a recent massive volume testifies, that moment has produced its own uninspiring professional impasse: an academicisation of popular culture that leaves one still in a spectatorial stance, facing yet again the issues of enablement and empowerment, of strategy and perspective. What now tends to be offered as alternatives to this old impasse are feminist criticism, with its alternatives to the received canon of both texts and paradigm practices, and some notion of 'postmodernist' criticism or theory. Both these proffered alternatives may, however, be only yet further variations on the basic pattern of the two earlier models: feminism as allocating a new group allegiance, yet locating oppression still in some underlying distribution of powers which needs prior reform before the more super-structural features of the oppressive universe are alterable; the postmodernists offering only updated formulae of totality, of ostensibly self-sustaining discursive formations which yet have to be somehow overturned or sabotaged by the very sustainers themselves.

If we want to think outside these parameters, if there is an emergent third model of 'theory' with some relation to what used to be literary theory, it may be useful to recall that earlier models of literary theory were connected to changes in two other fields: in literary production and in pedagogic practices. There was indeed a line that stretched from railways through three-decker novels to Leavis, just as there was also an overlap between the new poetry of modernism, the emphasis on individual teaching supervisions and the practice of close read-ing. If we now consider the significant literature of the past decade or so, it is arguable that one symptomatic genre has been cyberpunk fiction, as a focus for and articulation of several other developments, in hard science and in popular culture. Noticeably, it is one mode of writing that conflates both the areas omitted from Anderson's original map: fiction and hard science. It also directly connects to changes in the overall pedagogic situation, to the emergence of quite new technologies of social communication, information storage and intellectual production, themselves part of the social and indus-trial shifts which undermined both older class allegiances and the binary global oppositions of the Cold War epoch. The trains of the nineteenth-century industrial revolution are finally being replaced by the faxlines and satellite computer communication networks of the late twentieth century. Neither Marx nor Saussure can easily cope. By now this information revolution is no longer a matter for speculation or spectatorship even by literary academics, but deeply constitutive of the position we occupy precisely as academics and also as citizens. For what is at stake in these new developments is another epochal change in relations between knowledge and power, including those defining the status of the academy within a wider society.

We can single out three elements characteristic of the cyberpunk genre and its associated scientific developments. One is the dissolution of previous distinctions and divisions in computer design itself between hardware and software, with the 'connectionist' model of computer seeking to incorporate self-modifying neural networks to enable a learning process to occur through use rather than (as with any *langue: parole* model) the hardwiring of generalised rules upon which to operate specific application routines. The basic model here is the human brain itself. Second is the notion of the matrix, the shared information space accessible to any participant. By jacking into the computer networks, thereby joining the brain's own neural net into that of the matrix, the cyberrider effaces that other distinction between human and machine, and potentially therefore that between intellectual and manual labour which, for example, underpins the binary distinctions still deployed in that opening passage from Eagleton. Third, within the matrix, as with any hyperorganised system, the end of linearity is inevitable. Connections are no longer necessarily hierarchically structured but mappable as potential cross-linkings which conform to no previously prescribed or authorised pathways. The matrix explorer thus becomes an interactive agent rather than a follower of routes established by precedents or instructors. The moral panic aroused by hacking has its unavoidable basis here.

These features of the new information pattern have direct implications for pedagogy, some of which are already operative at primary and secondary levels, if not in most university English departments. What is involved is a real change in relations of authority and knowledge within pedagogy. If students now have desktop access to far more information than any teacher can hope to know or check, if the entire Library of Congress can now, or shortly, sit on a few CD-ROMS in a work cubicle, how can accredited knowledge status and formal expertise be exercised as control? And if the received hierarchies of organisation of knowledge are open to multiple modification through personalised search and retrieval routines, how can any canon or discipline of relevance be effectively maintained? Already in primary and secondary schools the advent of the personal computer has redefined the classroom task more as one of guidance in use of resources for searching out knowledge than as transmitting intellectual content.

(*A friend teaching in a small rural school in the United States writes that the school has just bought, for toddler use, more Apple Macintosh computers than my university's computing lab has.*)

One could, of course, link these developments back to older issues. The proliferation of computer networks, bulletin boards and electronic mail facilities might raise again the possibility of forms of public sphere, of non-territorial equal-access communication communities. The development of virtual reality technologies echoes some of the concerns of the Surrealists. The overlap between advanced computer research and immediate applications in the leisure and entertainment fields poses questions about the relation between popular and elite cultures: is learning the Amiga games-programming program Amos an elite educational activity or a street hobby? Brecht's account in *Galileo* of the dockyard mechanic instructing the philosopher in new methods of calculation might be recalled here. To some extent these developments can also recast our sense of previous forms of communication, storage and expression: we might now see the organising structure of Herbert's *The Temple* as that of a hypertext, or recognise the intense reading of a novel as an early form of jacking into a shared cyberspace or virtual reality, while some scholars have seen medieval uses of memory as akin to our own deployment of AI machines. The Hypercard program given away with every Macintosh computer can familiarise users with concepts of intertextuality and polyphonic reading that might once have figured in a seminar on Derrida. It was pleasantly predictable that Coleridge should figure as patron of some of these developments: Ted Nelson has named his proposed universal hyperbook 'Xanadu'. For just as one might see some older literature in these new terms, so these new developments can be seen as indebted to long-familiar modes of literary composition and comprehension: much modernist writing has already explored postlinear, polyphonic modes of organisation and of understanding; *The Waste Land*, as Ike Achebe has neatly shown, was always a kind of multimedia hypertext. The spatial form of the nineteenth-century novel itself could even be seen as anticipating the virtual acres of multiply-interconnecting databases. The notion of the matrix can be related to T.S. Eliot's insistence on having the whole of European art in one's very bones, while his notion of individual talent as effecting a shift in the internal relations of every pre-existing text can now be realised in the dynamic update features of multitasking operating systems.

(*One student of mine has found it easy and logical to move from research on reading strategies in* Finnegans Wake *to designing human-computer interfaces in a research lab.*)

In this brave new cyberworld some of the once merely ancillary skills taught on EngLit degree courses may now move more centre stage. The discipline of bibliographical citation extends into online database searching; with scanners and optical character recognition the problems of sloppy note-taking and of plagiarism are transmuted into concerns that echo Benjamin's dream of a text entirely composed of quotations; the writing of coursework essays becomes the composing of multimedia scripts. Educational production increasingly joins hands with those enjoyable forms of prosumer home production: video-editing and electronic music composition, bedroom studio-recording and public domain software-programming. Once students are encouraged by the very storage mechanisms available to them to create their own idiosyncratic interconnections rather than follow structured reading lists and syllabuses, the contribution of the teacher fades and with it those related hierarchies of theory and practice, the prioritising of preliminary theoretical clarification and allegiance. What replaces them may be only the simple but difficult awareness of the dense multitude of possible uses and reformulations of any text, including one's own wordprocessed rewrite of it.

There is of course an immediate and unwelcome political context within which some of these changes are currently being introduced into the educational system, by a government anxious to cheapen education in every sense, to cram undergraduate degrees into two years, to increase staff:student ratios and reduce research facilities. More widely, only a small percentage even of the developed world has these technologies available and endorsement of these directions can seem a matter solely of parochial privilege. Yet it is only ten years since the BBC introduced the first schools computer and a mere six or so since the user-friendly Mac interface appeared. The pace of innovation and penetration has been remarkable. The whole of Greek and Latin literature, including translations and lexicons, together with, for example, detailed maps and visual information on archaeological sites, can now be accessed on interactive laser disc. Much of English literature can now be downloaded in machine readable form. Secondary school pupils can now edit and publish on e-mail a European-wide school newspaper. Precisely because new pedagogic practices always underpin new theories, it is premature to extrapolate to the new theories likely to emerge in the near future, but involved in these technical possibilities is potentially a real transformation, beyond the limited priorities and perspectives of a cost-cutting government. Historically, revolutions involve a deep change in perceptions of the world and in taken-for-granted premisses, and these recent technical possibilities do imply a set of shifts on a par with those associated with the invention of print, perhaps even a change in human self-perception as far-reaching as the decentring of heliocentric man, as our notion of intelligence shifts to accommodate artificial intelligence. The materialism of the 1970s put the material body, of sexuality and biology, on to the political agenda, but the material structure of the brain itself is now crucial to the new developments.

Williams actually began *The Long Revolution* with an attempt to understand the notion of creativity in terms of J.Z. Young's work on the brain. He would presumably now begin from the more recent work on neural nets. If there is an underlying 'theory', that is perhaps where to locate it. But, in increasingly actual practice, the perspective available to us now is of an even longer revolution than Williams's, one in which at a point beyond current criteria of material sufficiency we can move towards a form of accessible electronic wealth, of values and pleasures located in information access and production. Even within the brief history and current limitations of the hardware, tens of millions already have personal computers that do not simply keep accounts or wordprocess but can play games, make music, paint, capture images and sounds. What was once the preserve of a few specialists in the various fields is now available even on the shelves of W.H. Smith. The latest issue of *Amiga Shopper* includes a program for constructing your own neural network. Within a few years the everyday games machine may be as powerful as today's SUN workstation, the domestic video recorder as sophisticated as the professional Sony systems in broadcast use now. When writing interactive online fiction is as common a practice as taking family snaps, or composing multitrack music is no more mysterious than dialling a telephone number, then 'literature' will perhaps have finally lost its last aura and become a genuinely secular, and democratic, activity. In the medieval monastery to read a text was to transcribe it, meditatively, for a month or more. That practice survived the printing press no more successfully than reading five-hundred-page novels on the train will outlast the laptop.

(*George Eliot, so the story goes, had tears running down her cheeks as she persisted with the translation of Strauss's* Life of Jesus, *knowing that the object of her faith was dissolving under her pen. She would look up from her desk to the crucifix upon her wall and pray to the Christ whose life was being demythologised by her own work. As I write this on my home computer I can see the books I write on it fading into antiquity even as I write them.*)

TRAVELLING THEORY

The train is moving again. Looking out of the window I am aware of the continuing deep influence of a certain reading of Marx. What I see is not only a natural beauty but worked land deeply formed by generations of labour, the material world as human product. As the train travels through that laboured land I recall Williams's texts on city and country, on known and unknown communities, his plays about the railways his father worked on in Pandy, with Tintern Abbey a few miles away. But now, with a changed attention, I find myself looking much more within the carriage, at the other people around me, and particularly at the children, aware of them too as the products of a certain kind of sustained and difficult labour, each child as formed not only from parental labour but as the end product of an immensely long yet also incredibly specific history, older than the most ancient heritage: the unique combination of a particular double lineage of DNA, of an unrepeatable configuration of neural nets and of a densely detailed personal history knowable only, if at all, in the strange territories of individual psychoanalysis. What is then profoundly ironic in the present context of government education policy, ostensibly preoccupied with economising and productivity, with waste of public resources and inefficient use of plant, is the immense waste of these incredibly sophisticated biocomputers, equipped with a nanotechnology older than empires and more powerful than a super Cray computer. These individual people, including me and my children, are the most extraordinary resource any community could want, yet the social formation that shapes us also wastes our immense potential of uniqueness.

Old habits die hard. I idly elaborate an insight into ideology: that all infants really have to believe that the world makes sense, since they are actually making sense of it as they grow – the development of their brain's neural network allows them no alternative; thus, given the kinds of actual environment children may have to make sense of, any system at all, however bizarre, can become the truth for them, even the paranoid culture and profligate economy of commodity capitalism. Perhaps, after all, education and family upbringing, those traditional emphases of the Right, are indeed more crucial than such relatively variable factors as the role of the working class or the function of intellectuals. Class, after all, is not only where you come from but where your kids are going. Yet the present social structure is so patently unstable and unpredictable, the present pace of scientific and technological development so rapid and unforeseeable, that it is even more impossible now to forecast where one's kids might one day find themselves. Railways opened up a new expanse of geographical mobility; my own working-class generation saw a new range of social mobility; now, my children will have available to them as a future form of mobility a kind of cyberspace travel that I can barely conceive.

The urgent agenda in my view, therefore, concerns not the elaboration of yet another theory of literary production or practice but the provision of an entire education appropriate to a generation who will outlive our very notions of intelligence, information, education. Older theories tended to be correlated with certain models of both pedagogy and writing. The first, basically economistic, model of theory often had its practical counterpart in the claim that what is wrong with education is a lack of resources. If only we could get the economy right, or enough teachers, or enough computers, then the students would follow, either in appropriate numbers (the government's concern) or desirable quality. A parallel with certain writing practices might be suggested, where the concern was to invest in a lifetime labour of scholarship and research before venturing to offer a cautious critical interpretation, or, at undergraduate level, to do the 'period' properly before you could understand the poem. I once wrote a hundred pages on one brief poem by Yeats; eighty of them were about the economic history of Ireland.

The second model of theory went with, or goes with, a situation in which teaching centres primarily on a text (literary or itself theoretical), now offered without reference to any specific historical context and often taught by a teacher who has no specific responsibility for the institutional context of that teaching. A fairly widespread model now in the States is that of the visiting guru parachuting in to give a prestige seminar or lecture series; this often produces what I think of as helicopter theory. The writing practice correlative to this theoretical stance tends to offer self-sustaining verbal icons as the preferred product model. I once wrote a five hundred page book which essentially held itself up by a number of internal dialectical structures. I then wrote a small book that included a variety of texts which had no reality other than that given by their imagined reviews in a fictive journal. Both books formally incorporated a dominant institutional device, and though I hope readers derived some pleasure and amusement, I doubt if either book was ever of much use to anyone.

The third model, or lack of one, that I want to propose is more like the bricolage of the home-video enthusiast who has to put together the bedroom computerised editing suite with whatever connections, leads, adapters and cables are to hand; the pedagogical equivalent is allowing students to become adept at constructing their own multidisciplinary curriculum, designed not for now but for about twenty years into an unknowable future. The writing component of such work is not the publishing of books but the drafting of degree programmes and course outlines. The proliferation of new degree courses and programmes, at Kent and elsewhere, seems increasingly the right area into which to put one's energies.

How, then, should I write this contribution to the state of theory? As an elaborated theoretical justification of that stance? As simply a list of resources? As an outline of a particular degree structure? Or perhaps, in deference to an older mode, as a meditative reflection, itself a kind of neural net, taking shape on a journey, a structure for discoveries rather than a predigest of conclusions, not so much a history or narrative as a frame for a few anecdotes, themselves nodes for new connections, switches and signals, repetitions and variations, weighted interlinkages, semantic nets, hidden layers? The neural net offers no single command economy, no organising consciousness over and above the net itself. The hardest task of all, pedagogically, theoretically, politically, may be to abandon the old radical desire for totalisation while not falling back into a parochially pragmatic concern or a tamed and muted area of special interest (literary theory 1968–90); rather, to design an open structure which recognises that precisely because 'Literature' was always, potentially, about everything, a 'literary' education now might involve work not just on narrative but on nuclear power, not only on women writers but on neural nets, not just on spatial form but on hyperspace. The equivalent of 'literary theory' might then be simply a set of enabling navigation tools, a backpack for cultural production.

One of the great strengths of Raymond Williams, in face-to-face teaching, was his refusal of the familiar temptation to take off from a student's hesitant contribution and magisterially to elaborate an extended insight from it. Instead he would characteristically respond to a student comment by listening carefully and then beginning quite elsewhere, only to work his way gradually and clearly back to the student's own final point, now leaving it open again for a different articulation and elaboration.

(*The train was finally drawing into London. I thought again of George Eliot, arriving at her changing metropolis, then of her own metaphors of webs and networks, her simile* (Middlemarch, ch. 38) *of random scratches brought into apparent concentric order by the arbitrary placing of a lamp. I was, as it happens, returning from my father's funeral and all the lights fell a little different now. I put Terry's* Theory *away in my case, tucked the copy of* Byte *under my arm, and jumped on to the platform.*)

APPENDIX: COMMUNICATIONS AND IMAGE STUDIES: DEGREE OUTLINE

Year 1

First and second terms, two one-term courses: seminar course, introduction to CIS; and skills course, introduction to image technology (video, computers).

Plus courses chosen from the full range of humanities courses, e.g. film narrative, historiography of art, linguistics, computing and humanities, courses from history, literature, theology, etc.

Third term: seminar course, 'Pop, porn, pulp and politics'; and skills course, photography workshop.

Part II

Year 2 core course: critical issues in communications.

Year 3 core course: history and theory of imaging.

Plus in each year three of the following: reading the image; the photograph; everyday images; images of identity, community and nation; modernity; other people, other places; media, culture and society; linguistics; image technology; option course (see list); project or dissertation (year 3 only).

Options

Film: film theory; early film form; British cinema; documentary; cinema and comedy; non-narrative cinema; sexual difference in cinema; fantastic film.

History and theory of art: art criticism; mannerism; the primitive; abstraction and construction; art and architecture of the Renaissance; patronage and cultural organisation.

Social sciences: political communication and mass media; propaganda, art and politics; social communications; systems of ritual and belief.

Computing: information technology; electronic publishing.

Drama: radio drama; playwriting; twentieth-century British theatre; women in theatre.

Literature/Language: literature, culture and society; literature and criticism; beginnings of literacy; explorations in English language; rhetoric and history in the classical world; landscape and the idea of England; comedy: text and theory; image, text and performance in the nineteenth century; sex, gender and society in the seventeenth century.

Philosophy: theory of knowledge; philosophy of mind; aesthetics; critical theory; philosophy and psychoanalysis; philosophy in literature.

SUGGESTED READINGS AND RESOURCES

These titles are given in a pedagogically useful order of consultation.

Williams, Raymond (1961) *The Long Revolution*, London: Chatto & Windus.
Anderson, Perry (1992) *English Questions*, London: Verso.
Eagleton, Terry (1990) *The Significance of Theory*, Oxford: Blackwell.
Eagleton, Terry (1984) *The Function of Criticism*, London: Verso.
Grossberg, L., Nelson, C. and Treichler, P. (eds) (1992) *Cultural Studies*, New York: Routledge.

Young, J.Z. (1964) *A Model of the Brain*, Oxford: Clarendon.
Hills, W. Daniel (1985) *The Connection Machine*, Cambridge, Mass.: MIT Press.
Aleksander, Igor and Burnett, Piers (1987) *Thinking Machines*, Oxford: Oxford University Press.
Kurzweil, Raymond (ed.) (1990) *The Age of Intelligent Machines*, Cambridge, Mass.: MIT Press.
Lycan, William G. (ed.) (1990) *Mind and Cognition*, Oxford: Blackwell.
Boden, Margaret (1990) *The Creative Mind*, London: Weidenfeld & Nicolson.
Davalo, Eric and Naim, Patrick (1991) *Neural Networks*, London: Macmillan Education.
Dennett, Daniel C. (1992) *Consciousness Explained*, London: Allen Lane.
Rucker, Rudy (1987) *Mind Tools*, New York: Houghton Mifflin.

Rucker, Rudy (1989) *Wetware*, London: Hodder & Stoughton.
Gibson, William (1984) *Neuromancer*, London: Gollancz.
Gibson, William (1986) *Burning Chrome*, London: Gollancz.
Gibson, William (1986) *Count Zero*, London: Gollancz.
Gibson, William (1988) *Mona Lisa Overdrive*, London: Gollancz.
Gibson, William and Sterling, Bruce (1992) *The Difference Engine*, London: Gollancz.

Carruthers, Mary (1990) *The Book of Memory*, Cambridge: Cambridge University Press.
Eisenstein, Elizabeth (1979) *The Printing Press as an Agent of Change*, Cambridge: Cambridge University Press.
Brand, Stewart (1988) *The Media Lab*, Harmondsworth: Penguin.
Nielsen, Jakob (1990) *Hypertext and Hypermedia*, London: Academic Press.
Rheingold, Howard (1991) *Virtual Reality*, London: Summit Books.
Benedikt, Michael (ed.) (1991) *Cyberspace*, Cambridge, Mass.: MIT Press.
Hayward, Philip (ed.) (1990) *Culture, Technology and Creativity*, London: John Libbey.
Ross, Andrew (1991) *Strange Weather*, London: Verso.
Kinder, Marsha (1991) *Playing with Power*, Berkeley, Calif.: University of California Press.

Guy Wright (1991) *Amiga Desktop Video Power*, Grand Rapids, Mich.: Abacus.

Philip Gladwin (1992) 'Build a brain' parts 1, 2, and 3 in *Amiga Shopper*, 14,15,16.

Ike Achebe *The Waste Land* hypertext disc (Coventry University).

Oxford University Computing Service 'Text archive' (ARCHIVE- @UK.AC.OXFORD.VAX).

CTI Centre for Textual Studies 'Resources guide' (CTITEXT@UK- .AC.OX.VAX).

2

THEORY AND DIFFICULTY

Thomas Docherty

Theory is 'difficult'; teaching theory is perhaps more so; and, for some, teaching 'literature' through a reading inflected in the language of theory is virtually impossible. The frequency with which one hears the suggestion that 'this stuff just cannot be taught' is surprising, in a profession where the development of strategies for 'teaching' unfamiliar materials is essential. To say that theory is so difficult that it cannot be taught is, of course, either simply stupid and unprofessional, or (much more likely) it is a tacit strategy in a theoretical position which does not wish its own theoretical assumptions to be exposed and discussed.

No less surprising is the tacit suggestion in this position that 'poetry' (or literature in general) is any less 'difficult'. The merest glimpse at any widely used anthology of literary texts demonstrates abundantly clearly that the language typically used by poets is obscure, indirect, problematic and entirely unsuited to pragmatic communication as we currently understand it. Yet, pedagogically, the institution has usually prided itself on making the difficulties of poetry evaporate, on making it 'accessible' to a recalcitrant readership, that is, students, who know but who are not permitted to acknowledge the axiomatic, structural function of poetry's obscurities. To pass an examination is to demonstrate a (real or pretended) intellectual mastery – which may of course reveal itself in entirely unpredictable ways – over one's texts. In this state of affairs, even the reader's suggestion that a specific text 'resists' adequate comprehension becomes acceptable as an indication of a specific mastery: the acknowledgement of difficulty has become, paradoxically, a mark of the greater intellect of a reader who is unsatisfied with 'superficial' comprehension. In short, the acknowledgement of difficulty is itself, in the pedagogical institution, a tactic in the demonstration of the fundamental simplicity and accessibility of the text.

None the less, it would be misleading to deny that the complexities of a broad 'theory' had added new and specific difficulties to the practices of literary study, most obviously in the field of 'English' where many a doughty battle has been fought in recent years. These battles might succinctly be described in terms borrowed from Robert Scholes: some would suggest that we should abandon the practice of 'teaching literature', replacing it with a more sceptical practice of 'studying texts' (Scholes 1985). The distinction is that between 'appreciation' and 'criticism', between a positive evaluation of literary texts and a threateningly negative evaluation. The appearance of such a tension in the institution has disturbed the otherwise smooth flow and passage of literary knowledge from writer to teacher to reader. This situation is further complicated by the economic and political circumstances of the academic institution in Western Europe, which have determined that the university will emulate the efficiency model of capitalist industry, manufacturing a 'product' (the educated student) which can be safely and easily located in the wider workforce of the social formation.

This is where the specificity of this problem in 'English' becomes apparent. As a discipline, 'English' threatens to become particularly vacuous. Its subject-matter has been less precisely definable than the subject-matter of French (language and civilisation) or of physics (force and matter), and so on. 'English' has often been considered implicitly as a kind of complement to the otherwise fully 'cerebral' work of the academy. Its unstated task has been to deliver and produce a specific historical subject whose function is the internalisation and subsequent vigorous legitimation of the dominant ideological norms of her or his social formation. Literary texts, widely construed as being about 'human nature', are thus the excuse for this tacit practice of value-formation. Since its inception as a university discipline, English literature has been both the repository and the producer of the cultural norms of the anglophone world. It is always threatened by a dangerous conservative lack of criticism.

The structure I outline here bears an intended resemblance to the structure of the *Bildungsroman* elucidated by Franco Moretti in *The Way of the World* (Moretti 1987). In the classic novel of development, the central character begins from a position of something like alienation: she or he is not fully an integral part of the social formation. The very immaturity or under-development of the character means that she or he cannot fully and firmly 'fit into' or play an identifiable part in the workings of the society which the character observes. The *Bildungsroman* is above all a novel determined by time: but the character must use her or his time in order to discover the best way of becoming a legitimate part of the social formation which she or he experiences as being merely 'adjacent' to themselves. Such a metonymic relationship has to become thoroughly metaphorical. This means that the character has to use her or his time not just to critique the society but also to learn and, indeed, to internalise its basic ideological norms. At that point, she or he finds an entry point into the society – most often by the door marked 'marriage'. The character now espouses the familial and other norms of the society; and, in turn, the society accords the character the full recognition and legitimacy which she or he desired in the first place. Metaphorically – indeed allegorically – the character and the society 'represent' each other to each other. My argument here is that contemporary life reiterates this kind of fiction at a different ontological level: for *Bildungsroman*, read 'English literature university course'. Hamlet, the revenger at Elsinore, has given up the antic disposition for the reasonable contemporary disposition of the student from Wittenberg. This way, a bridge into the social formation is crossed, and Hamlet the student may find an entirely different (if much less critical) response to his intolerable society and to his own difficult and unhappy situation.

How might we return a properly critical act to 'English'? Can its implicit conservatism be challenged? I propose to answer this in the affirmative. Yet I will not suggest that 'theory' as such is any less conservative than 'English'; rather, if the possibility of criticism lies anywhere, it lies in 'difficulty' itself. It is to this that I now turn directly.

ON CRITICISM AS LIMINALITY

George Steiner (1978) formulated four types of difficulty in poetry: contingent, modal, tactical and ontological. Contingent difficulties are those faced when we simply do not recognise a word or the meaning of an allusion in a phrase: we must therefore 'look it up' in an exercise Steiner regards as the inevitability of incessant 'homework'. This will help us find out, for instance, what a 'ptyx' is when we come across it in Mallarmé. Modal difficulties arise when there is a significant discrepancy between the manner in which a poem may be 'cerebrally' available to us while yet remaining 'emotionally' distanced, when (as Steiner has it) 'we cannot coerce our own sensibility into the relevant frame of perception' (Steiner 1978: 33). When there is an obscurity in the poem's language or a sense that language is inadequate to the situation it purports to describe, we are in the realm of tactical difficulties, which 'endeavour to deepen our apprehension by dislocating and goading to new life the supine energies of word and grammar' (ibid.: 40). These are those more immediately irritating difficulties when we suspect that a poet is being wilfully obscure.

All three of these categories of difficulty presuppose the possibility or even the necessity of poetry as an intelligible act. The fourth category, the ontological difficulty identified by Steiner, arises when the assumption of some kind of commensurability between the language of the poet and the language of the audience is no longer taken for granted, when the contract of communicability is broken. Although Steiner proposes it as his final category, it seems obvious to me that this difficulty underpins all the others. 'Homework' or the 'coercion of sensibility' and so on are, in fact, just so many strategies for the recuperation of an ideal of communicability which poetry exists to contest. As Steiner has it, 'Lexical resistance is the armature of meaning, guarding the poem from the necessary commonalities of prose' (ibid.: 21). If we take Steiner at face value, 'difficulty' can always be overcome in some way. But if we put all difficulty under the sign of the ontological difficulty, we then open the possibility of the insuperable difficulty in poetry, with the consequence that we must call into question the kind of 'sovereign subject' of comprehension which seems so desirable to Steiner and to an academy founded upon the aesthetic construction of the *Bildungsroman*.

In the teaching situation, the most basic problem is the common tacit acceptance of the proposition that the written text is 'redundant'. For a number of (no doubt valid) pedagogical reasons and a number of (no doubt invalid) ideological reasons, students begin their work in the institution of literary studies assuming that the poem is but the vehicle of something more important and fundamental, which is conceived either as its message (what it says, regardless of medium), or as their own message (what they can say about it). For many if not most students, poetry is a form of communication and, despite McLuhan, the message is strongly felt to be more important than the medium.

Poetry, we might say, exists in this model as a peculiar form of deferred intimacy between reader and writer. The primary reason for the deferral of intimacy is quite simply the relative 'belatedness' of the reader, who always comes to the poet's message 'too late' and who, as a result, cannot fully understand its content. Hence the prevalence of the idea of criticism as liminality. Like a helpful tour-guide, this criticism inserts itself precisely on the threshold between artist and reader, and interprets the message. We are at once given access to the artistic monuments of an antic or antique world this way, but unfortunately this access is given by someone standing in front of the monument and partly blocking our view of it. We gain a message; we lose the poem; we cannot trust the messenger. This is unsatisfactory and self-contradictory (Eagleton 1976).

As a model, this also places the teacher in the position of tour-guide: the teacher becomes the real bridge between writer and reader, making herself or himself indispensable to the reader precisely at the moment of revealing the text's redundancy. The employability of the teacher is at the cost of the redundancy of poetry in this scheme. Consequently, of course, there arises a hint of a self-serving and self-legitimating authority in the figure of the teacher here. If the teacher is the only such bridge (that is, if all poetry has to be thus mediated), this authority can slip easily (though not necessarily) into authoritarianism.

The fundamental problem with the criticism-as-bridge metaphor is its prioritisation of a spatial metaphor which assumes a distance and a barrier between writer and reader. Hence the necessity, as Dante acknowledged, of a Virgilian teacher who can introduce a foreign world of alterity to the domestic concerns of a reader. The spatialisation of thinking here contributes fundamentally to the constitution of what Bourdieu refers to as an 'aristocracy of culture' (Bourdieu 1984: ch. 1). This is an important matter, for it brings together the idea of legitimation with the notion of time and personal development identified in my characterisation of the academy as structural *Bildungsroman*. It requires further elucidation.

As Bourdieu indicates, aristocracies are 'essentialist', and accordingly they function differently from meritocracies and other sociocultural and political systems in terms of legitimation. The meritocrat, for instance, finds herself or himself legitimised in relation to some ostensibly objective (or consensually agreed) measure. Legitimation here is dependent upon what the meritocrat does. Contrary to this, the aristocrat requires no external legitimation: she or he finds that an activity is legitimate not by virtue of any doing, but rather by virtue of being. That is, the aristocracy finds itself legitimised by virtue simply of its being aristocratic. In matters of aesthetics, the 'taste' of the aristocracy of culture need never be explained – and, indeed, cannot be explained. For taste to require explication is itself already a demonstration of an intrinsic vulgarity in the aesthetic predisposition of the critic.

In 'literary appreciation', it is necessarily assumed that there exists an inner core of essential meaning which inheres not in the text but somewhere more evanescent, in the consciousness or unconscious of the poet. That core is immediately accessible to an aristocracy of culture who thus intuit or feel directly the value of the text as an adequate reflection or focus of such meaning. In pedagogy, this core has been accessed by a teacher, but not yet – that is, not immediately – by a reader. Mediative interpretation thus sets up not only the principle of accessibility but also, and correspondingly, the principle of an unmediated vision, possessed by poet and cultural aristocrat. In short, the desire for accessibility carries within itself an acknowledgement of exclusivity as a formative principle of communication.

In criticism as an exercise in liminality, the fundamental arrangement is established between an aristocracy of culture who are able immediately to 'appreciate' positively the text being discussed, and a group of excluded readers who wish to gain access to such 'taste', but whose vulgarity ensures that they require mediation. Such mediation implies a temporal discrepancy between, on the one hand, the cultural aristocrat as charismatic teacher and, on the other, the tardy and under-developed reader. We have a structure here which precisely locates the reader as 'immature'; her or his maturity will then depend, as in the structure of the *Bildungsroman*, upon an internalisation of certain values to the point where they appear to become reflex, immediate, axiomatic and essential. When such values are unquestioned, when they become a ground for all future reading or any subsequent thinking, then the readers have 'matured' aesthetically and politically. Their statements about a text acquire legitimacy not through relation to any external or theoretical measure, but rather precisely because they become self-serving. We call this process *Bildung*, forma-tion, education. Criticism has begun to evaporate here, for there is no requirement of an external or objective validation of one's 'taste'; theory has also been declared redundant, for theory is precisely such an explicatory grounding or founda-tional philosophy upon which one's aesthetic comments are based. All that remains is distinction, between those inside the realm of proper self-legitimising and essential social or human values and those immature or under-developed who are con-demned by their vulgarity to remain illegitimate or to gain recognition and legitimacy through conformity.

The very idea of criticism as a bridge, of criticism as media-tion or as the making available of a material which is for whatever reason 'difficult', is thus complicit with a politics of essentialism, a politics which can serve only the aristocracy of culture. Accessibility is itself part of the problem for an attitude which would want to remain vigilantly critical, rather than blandly conformist or mature. If this is so, then we must reconsider liminality and difficulty.

The *limen* is, like a river, like a hymen, a double-edged entity. It both joins and separates at once. If criticism is a liminal bridge between essential meaning and baffled reader, then it is always possible to refuse to cross the bridge. It is possible to refuse collaboration with a politics based upon an aesthetics of 'taste' or aesthetic appreciation. It is possible to begin from an acknowledgement of the potentially insuperable difficulty of comprehension.

To cross the bridge is to fall into complicity with a theoretical stance which produces not knowledge but only recognition. Two things are involved in such neo-romantic 're-cognition'. First, the words of the critic are 'recognised' in the sense that they are regarded as legitimate and available for hearing. If they are controversial, they are so only within parameters of agreement and consensus established as the boundaries of legitimate discourse within the consensually agreed social formation. They must remain within such boundaries if they are to be recognisable at all. Hence the recognisable becomes, in fact, the domesticated, the controllable. Second, the world proposed by the critic is re-cognised. That is to say, the words of the critic are only legitimate if they re-present the world as it is, in its would-be essential being. At this point, of course, the very idea of knowledge as something which is cumulative begins to disintegrate. Knowledge has been reduced to the merest anamnesis and there is, in the cognitive field, nothing new under the sun. The world is as it is and cannot be any other way.

Such recognition is, therefore, inherently conservative and anti-historical. The notion of a temporal development – the historical procedures implicit in the structure of *Bildung*, formation – is countered and controlled by a predominant impetus towards a spatial organisation in which the critic finds her or his proper place in the world's spatial arrangement of inner aristocratic core and outer realm of vulgar darkness. The possibility of cognitive disruption must be re-established if we are to maintain the possibility not only of criticism but also of history itself.

ON SPEED AND DIFFICULTY

The difference between aristocratic immediacy and vulgar mediation is, of course, a difference of speed. It is here that, as Virilio (1977) helps indicate, the fundamental issue of such a cultural politics resides. The *Bildung* model of criticism addressed above has two central components: it constructs criticism as a personalist and basically therapeutic exercise in self-development; it conspires to ignore the temporal and historical component of difficulty in the relation between writer and reader, in the text. If we attend more pedantically to difficulty, then it becomes possible to retard the overly premature collapsing of the political into the personal implicit in *Bildung* and, correspondingly, it enables us to attend to the properly historical difficulty of reading.

It will be objected here that I am driving a wedge between the personal and the political in such a way as to sever the political from the concerns of everyday cultural and social practice. I therefore restate the key term in my formulation: premature. In this argument, I do not object to the bringing together of the personal (or social) and the political; but I do object to the premature collapsing of one into the other which enables us completely to ignore the personal or the social in their own specificities. Criticism has been far too brusquely 'politicised' in an extremely banal manner. While agreeing absolutely that criticism exists within and through political formations, I can and do still object to the willed ignorance of criticism in the interests of talking about politics in a manner which is ill informed and often irrelevant to the critical and aesthetic matters to hand. In the wake of Benjamin's warning about the aestheticisation of politics (Benjamin 1973), the drive to the politicisation of aesthetics has been not just too brisk but also too simple, not difficult enough. Difficulty, I argue, must be embraced if for no other reason than that it will slow us down, that it will forbid prematurity.

Immediacy, as favoured by the aristocracy of culture, tries to deny time altogether and relocates the relations between reader and text in the spatial terms discussed above. It is a strategic mistake, for a criticism that would be historical and radical, to accede to the spatial metaphor and make a plea for accessibility. Simply to locate more readers on the inside of the aristocracy of culture is, in effect, to defuse further the possibility of a radical criticism at all. It may empower certain individuals, but in wrong, reactionary and individualist or essentialist ways. The time of mediation has to be acknowledged fully, and this brings us to the fundamental issue of historical difficulty.

The first two kinds of difficulty in poetry examined by Steiner are both, in a sense, historical. The contingent and the modal both arise when there is a significant discrepancy between contemporary culture and the cultural norms, as effected in and through language, of the poet. Translation of a sort is required, according to Steiner, if we are to counter these difficulties. The assumption, of course, is that a foreign discourse is domesticated in this exercise of simplificatory translation. But what if translation were to go the other way? What if we were to attend fully to the historical specificity of the text in all its alterity, and to strive to translate the terms of our culture back into those of a former or a foreign culture? The effect would be first to arrest the sense that the world – even in its ostensibly most intractably alien forms and languages – is available for consciousness. Further, the effect would be to preserve the text in its historical moment, its 'aura', to borrow Benjamin's term (1973: 223). The net result is a slowing down of the optimistic phenomenological process whereby through an act of hermeneutics the subject of consciousness appropriates the world as a mirror in which that subject is legitimated, its self-sufficiency and self-presence guaranteed. If the world is available for consciousness, then it is so, now, only in a manner in which the subject cannot presume a mastery or control over it. The subject, in short, is not 'centred', for the world is not thought in such spatial terms. In this set-up, the subject exists in and through time, which means that it can never be fully present to itself, never 'essential'; rather, it is fully conditioned by delay and by a temporality which is immune to 'immediacy'.

Steiner's third and fourth types of difficulty both explicitly produce 'slowness'; significantly, they do this by in a sense rejecting the assumption of the immediacy of apprehension within the text and by preserving the text as a discrete entity, separated from consciousness by a linguistic obscurity and maintained in its separate sphere of historical being. History thus becomes available precisely in the discrepancy between the moment of the text and the moment of its reading. The task of reading is, among other things, a maintenance of respect precisely for this historicity or this division between text and reader.

What if we abandon the normativity of the communicability or intelligibility principles in criticism? What if we start from an acknowledgement of the difficulty of reading 'across time', a difficulty compounded by the possibility of a severe and strict incommensurability between the language games deployed by the poet and the different language games available to us? It would follow from this that the norm would become one in which we could never assume that a text was available for consciousness at all. Such availability would be the result of reading and would, in an early Fishian sense, be the meaning of the activity of reading and, subsequently, the meaning of the text (Fish 1972). In a strict sense, this would also produce the possibility of a genuine act of cognition in criticism, a 'shock of the new' (Hughes 1980). But such cognition would also have to be fully acknowledged as a historical cognition, specific to its own historical moment and not necessarily available for straightforward reiteration or 're-cognition' by another reader. What we begin to witness here is the loss of consensus around a text and the production of the possibility of dissent. In short, we produce the possibility of radical and historical disagreement of a kind more radical than that suggested by Parrinder as the axiomatic principle of criticism in itself (Parrinder 1987).

The reader, at this point, is no doubt expecting me to produce 'theory' as just such a mechanism of complexification, as the answer to our historical and radical worries about criticism. Yet it would be true to say that theory has also been proposed, generally, as something which is more or less readily available. In some of its guises, theory is part of the uncritical problem.

There have been two possible tendencies for the development of theory within 'English' and associated cultural practices. The first of these, the tendency to move towards cultural studies or cultural politics, has (within those circles which will embrace theory at all) become dominant (Easthope 1991). This is the tendency which I identify as part of the problem.

The dominant theoretical mode in pedagogical terms, and in terms of the internal politics which afflicts the academy and institution, has been one which builds upon a fundamental subscription to semiotic analysis. The world is a sign system, of varying degrees of codification and complexity. Criticism will unmask such sign systems to reveal the fundamental powers and oppressions upon which the cultural sign – the political world – sustains itself. In this, two fundamental steps are always taken as a basic ground. First, material things are translated into signs; second, such signs are assumed to be available (more or less immediately) to consciousness and thus are assumed to be available for insertion into a system of signification. While accepting the theoretical proposition that these two steps may always be possible, it is none the less the case that, in practice, they are always taken prematurely. The 'thinginess' of the world – what the great proto-postmodernist Duns Scotus would regard as its *haecceitas* – is too quickly subsumed into a sign; and signs, it is always assumed, are – if not immediately then immanently – available for a peculiar domestication which we identify as understanding (and which, as I argue above, is better considered merely as consensual conformity).

Thus, for instance, I have heard it argued (and this had best remain anonymous: the type of argument will be instantly recognisable) that the Malvinas/Falklands War in 1982 was essentially a war about signifying practices and about discourses. This argument, of course, sustains itself only in the most pusillanimous and parochial terms: the discourse in question turns out in these circumstances to be that of Thatcherism, which was in a moment of crisis in Britain in 1982. There is no question either of the possibility that other, indeed foreign, discourses might carry on regardless of any such parochial debates, or of the fact that to a soldier staring down the barrel of a gun, discourse is probably the last thing to be on the tip of the tongue. But to the superannuated academic who is profoundly aware of her or his own political inefficacy, such an argument seems to be attractive for the simple reason that it makes the English teacher politically 'relevant', and relatively important. Yet this is precisely the identification of the charismatic or heroic teacher who sustains, as I demonstrated above, the conservative aristocracy of culture.

The more honest intellectual path, of course, is one which accepts that the event of war exists, in a specific ontological sense (though not necessarily in a semantic one) independently of discourse. The issue of mediatic representation might be of utmost importance (as in the more recent case of the Gulf War), but death on the Basra Road would have been death all the same even if it, like much of the war, had remained invisible. The 'thinginess' or, simply, the materiality of the historical world should be acknowledged first and foremost as something which may, at this historical and ontological level, be resistant to language and signification. Such a resistance, however, cannot be entertained in a situation where speed is of the essence, where it is incumbent on the reader that she or he find a kind of master-theory (semiotics) which, with numerous varied inflections, will collapse the entire history of the material world into a text that is immediately available for decoded comprehension.

One major difficulty with such a theoretical work is that it fails to account for the accidental (as opposed to the necessary). For instance, a cat suddenly runs in front of a speeding car and is struck by it. At one level, this is an event without meaning, or without intrinsic and immanent meaning. It will, of course, be inserted into a meaningful situation when, for instance, the owner of the cat is informed, or when the driver of the car feels sickened. But the accidental in itself carries no immanent significance: it is an event or a thing and not in the first instance a sign. My objection to the dominant 'cultural studies' model of theory is that it operates merely at the level of the more 'necessary' (that is, the intended) sign, and that in order to do this it either erases the accidental event or prematurely collapses it into a system of signification. Historically, such an event is more than and is different from the linguistic or alphabetic difference between the /t/ of 'cat' and the /r/ of 'car'. And this 'more', this excess, is not simply an excess of signification: it may be a more which is independent of language and of signification. It may, in short, be history.

How might we deal with this? It seems apparent that the only answer is one which is not immediately attractive. Not only must we acknowledge, for a start, the difficulties of poetry, we must also acknowledge the difficulties of theory. Further – and this is the part which will no doubt appear intolerable to some – we must use theoretical work in order to deepen further the complexity and difficulty of poetry: we must make texts more and more resistant to signification and allow them – even encourage – their full obscurity.

CONCLUSION

If theory is valuable, then, it is valuable precisely to the extent that it increases the difficulty of poetry and other cultural matters. As de Man famously argued (1986), the greatest resistance to theory stems from within theory itself; what he did not add was that the main cause of this was the desire for speed, or for the etymologically given sense of this word, for 'success', for mastery. The acknowledgement of difficulty, and the exacerbation of difficulty, will be useful in the inculcation of a critical attitude of a specific 'humility'. Instead of a masterful consciousness which assumes, in true optimistic fashion, that the world is available for consciousness here and now and that the 'I' here and now can (at least potentially if not in fact) masterfully comprehend it, we should encourage what Vattimo and Rovatti (1983) identify as *il pensiero debole*, a weak thinking, which, though 'weak', at least has the virtue of saving the honour of 'thinking'.

It is of no cultural use to endorse 'access' or 'accessibility' in poetry and theory. The sole effect of this is to give a greater number of people access to the social space of an entirely bogus aristocracy of culture. That aristocracy is self-sustaining: poetry, theory, will not sustain it, for both poetry and theory resist its inherent anti-historical essentialism. Given that poetry exists as a resistance to meaning, it also exists as a form of resistance to essentialism and to the philosophical optimism born of such essentialism. Poetry, like theory, is useful for a radical cultural or aesthetic politics precisely because it is, in a specific sense of the term, 'pessimistic'. Paradoxically perhaps, it is such pessimism, encouraged and endorsed by the increasing difficulty of theory, which is our only source of hope.

BIBLIOGRAPHY

Benjamin, Walter (1973) *Illuminations*, ed. Hannah Arendt, trans. Harry Zohn, Glasgow: Fontana/Collins.

Bourdieu, Pierre (1984) *Distinction*, trans. Richard Nice, London: Routledge & Kegan Paul.

de Man, Paul (1986) *The Resistance to Theory*, Manchester: Manchester University Press.

Eagleton, Terry (1976) *Criticism and Ideology*, London: New Left Books.

Easthope, Antony (1991) *Literary into Cultural Studies*, London: Routledge.

Fish, Stanley (1972) *Self-Consuming Artifacts*, Berkeley and Los Angeles: University of California Press.

Hughes, Robert (1980) *The Shock of the New*, London: BBC Books.

Moretti, Franco (1987) *The Way of the World*, London: Verso.

Parrinder, Patrick (1987) *The Failure of Theory*, Brighton: Harvester Press.

THOMAS DOCHERTY

Scholes, Robert (1985) *Textual Power*, London: Yale University Press.
Steiner, George (1978) *On Difficulty*, Oxford: Oxford University Press.
Vattimo, Gianni, and Pier Aldo Rovatti (eds) (1983) *Il Pensiero debole*, Milan: Feltrinelli.
Virilio, Paul (1977) *Vitesse et politique*, Paris: Galilée.

3

IN EXEMPLIFICATION

Steven Connor

Studies of the question of disciplinarity have tended to assume that the identity of a discipline is established and sustained principally in its designation and preservation of a particular field of objects – the literary text, the past, the artistic image, the physical space of the earth, the realm of speculative ideas – along with a set of protocols of argument and exposition. One of the most important, but rarely discussed, mediators between these two dimensions is exemplification. All intellectual disciplines requiring forms of public exposition (which is perhaps to say all intellectual disciplines whatsoever) must work by selective demonstration, illustration, case study, synecdoche: in short, by the strategic deployment of examples. The character, and claim to legitimacy, of a discipline is largely defined by the way it regulates the passage from example to generality.

This is to say more than that disciplines are characterised by the distinctive ways in which they use evidence, for there is an important difference between evidence and examples, evidencing and exemplification. Examples are different from evidence in that they occur not in the process of reasoning or research (whether or not one conceives this to be prior to or concurrent with the process of writing), but come to visibility in the presentation of that reasoning and research. The difference between evidence and exemplification is therefore the difference between enquiry and the articulation of that enquiry in some more or less organised, more or less institutional form. Exemplification is the mode by which a discipline instantiates itself, making itself known or present to itself and to others.

Exemplification usually operates in an indexical or synecdochic mode, by substituting the part for the whole. It is a way of economising on space, time and language, and perhaps as such an instance of that narrowing or 'rarefaction' of discourse described by Foucault (1981: 56). For the most part, this economic aspect is all we are aware of in the workings of exemplification: the need to save time, to choose the best, the most efficient examples, which will do the most work in the shortest time. Hence the familiar *topoi* of deferral, on the pattern of the following; 'constraints of time and space do not allow me to offer a full account of *a*; but, as a tentative beginning, I here offer as an example *b*.' Exemplification has the structure of a promise – which is to say that it draws the future into the grasp of the present, while at the same time deferring, even making doubtful, the arrival of that future. Exemplification also establishes a kind of promissory ratio; by standing as a part of a whole, the example always evokes and guarantees the whole from which it has been abstracted. The closeness of the words 'example' and 'sample' is instructive here, for the principle of the sample is the principle of representative homogeneity (it does not matter where you take your sample from in a homogeneous field or material, since it will constitute a miniature of the whole from which it has been taken.) Exemplification always suggests this kind of homogeneity; cutting into the body of the material to derive the sample both interrupts and guarantees the unity of the material. The extraction and display of examples are simultaneously totality's wound and cure.

Exemplification is therefore the means of articulation of a discipline, in both senses; it speaks the discipline, brings it to visibility, and it holds the discipline together, establishing its world, its history and its future. Influentially, but also misleadingly, Lyotard (1984) has suggested that the predominating mode of discursive legitimation for Western forms of knowledge is metanarrative. In fact, however, as Lyotard himself seems repeatedly to indicate t hough never to realise himself, it is not metanarrative as such which guarantees the legitimacy of any particular area of inquiry, but rather the agreed ways of showing how the work of a particular discipline exemplifies, illustrates and confirms the progress towards the singular goals of emancipation, spirit or freedom which lie at the end of metanarratives.

As the mode in which a discipline makes itself present to

itself, the work of exemplification is present in every compartment and activity of a discipline. Principles and protocols of exemplification are important, not only in research and published work more generally but in conference papers, lectures, dissertations, the structure of curricula, methods of examination, even in the mundanities of library purchasing and reading lists. All the norms and values of literary study, the processes of canon-formation and transmission, the protocols of good reading, depend upon a willingness, both shared and institutionally imparted, to fall in with the functions of the example. Exemplification is an endlessly renewed promise of the reciprocal conformity of theory and its object: a guarantee of the possibility and effectiveness of the procedures of argument and evidencing. And, most importantly of all, the manner in which a discipline or intellectual formation uses or approves its examples operates as a model for the kind of examples which may then seem adequate or allowable in that discipline. This is to say that the most important function of exemplification is to exemplify itself; exemplification works to establish models for the approved modes of exemplification instinct within any discipline. When a teacher stands before a class and discusses a text, or a portion of a text, that teacher is most importantly offering a homoeostatic model for the ways in which students themselves are to select and deploy examples.

Disciplines may be characterised by the following variables with regard to exemplification: ratio, or the question of how many examples are needed to make any particular argument plausible; substitutability, or the degree to which examples may tend or be held or be required to be interchangeable with one another, and therefore to enforce conviction through their accumulation (for some disciplines, the more examples that can exemplify the same thing in the same way, the better; for others, the more examples are multiplied, the less unified they may seem); typicality, or the question of how representative examples should be of the general conditions they exemplify; separability, or the degree to which examples may be seen as pure data, separable from or prior to hypotheses; and priority, or the question of the relative significance or authority of the example as compared to what it exemplifies. Disciplines may be distinguished not merely in terms of the fixed values which obtain in each of these areas, but also by the degree to which each of them may or may not be seen as a problem and the degree to which they are or are not seen as separable from each other.

What are the characteristic forms of exemplification in the discipline of English, or literary studies more generally? We might plausibly suggest that literary studies have typically been characterised by a strikingly low ratio of examples to proof – we are more inclined to accept a case about Romanticism, modernism or postmodernism that is demonstrated through a small number of examples than a historian would be in equivalent circumstances, and, indeed, there is little concept in literary studies of statistical significance; there is consequently a low degree of substitutability in the use of examples in literary studies. Literary studies seem also to have a relatively weak concern with typicality, and, in fact, often show a tendency to privilege the aberrant over the representative example. Correspondingly, literary studies encounter many problems in separating examples as data from the presuppositions which they do or do not confirm; indeed, one may say that the problems of the hermeneutic circle are not only congenital in but in some way also constitutive of Anglo-American literary studies. All of this seems to add up to a marked preference in literary studies for the example over the generality, even a sense that the purpose of general propositions is to provoke a more responsive account of the working of particular examples.

Indeed, it may be said that literary studies is the most exemplificatory of subjects, precisely because of its mistrust of fullness, total explanation or grand narrative. Although we may endlessly contract for the total account and even aspire and plan towards it in our research, writing and course design, there is something grotesque and monstrous for our discipline about such attempts to specify the workings of such totalities; this is the reason, perhaps, for the continuing indigestability of structuralist projects such as Propp's narratology of the folktale or Barthes' *The Fashion System* (1983), which not only apprehended but also attempted to literalise semiotic systems, spelling out their entire *combinatoire* of possibilities. In fact, it seems as though a principal characteristic of Anglo-American literary studies is their resistance to the completion of the passage from example to general statement, their preference for the erotics of lack, the pleasure, to borrow Barthes' analogy in *The Pleasure of the Text*, of the gaping garment, rather than the nifty buttoning down of example on exemplified (Barthes 1990: 9).

To explain this, we need to make a distinction between two different uses of the example, a distinction between what I would like to call exemplification and exemplarity. I have so far been discussing examples of exemplification, which is to say the agencies of the movement from the singular to the general, the element to the system, the syntagm to the paradigm, the *langue* to the *parole*, the detail to the whole, the case to the law. But literary studies have been dominated for most of this century by a professional ethic of exemplarity, which is to say the use of examples which retard or even resist the passage between these two dimensions. This practice derives largely from the Kantian doctrine of the non-conceptual nature of the aesthetic. The aesthetic object, Kant writes in his *Critique of Judgement*, cannot be governed by logical rules and precedents. If some work of art furnishes an example of artistic genius, it does so not by conforming to any sort of pattern but rather by instancing an exemplariness:

> The natural endowment of art . . . must furnish the rule, but what kind of rule must this be? It cannot be one set down in a formula and serving as a precept – for then the judgement upon the beautiful would be determinable according to concepts. Rather must the rule be gathered from the performance, i.e., from the product, which others may use to put their own talent to the test, so as to let it serve as a model, not for *imitation*, but for *following*.
> (Kant 1988: 170–1; original emphases)

Imitation is to following here as exemplarity is to exemplification. It is the difference between a model that provides a general rule and one that exemplifies its own unprecedented and inimitable exemplarity. It would be absurd to try to reduce Shakespeare, Kant would say, to a set of maxims and procedures, which might then be copied by other writers. The only things that Shakespeare could authentically exemplify would be his qualities of absolute unprecedentedness and inimitability. And yet this is intended in Kant to yield some generalisable principle, indeed one might think it intrinsic to a definition of aesthetic value that it be so generalisable. As

Derrida has remarked, commenting on Kant's notion of non-conceptual exemplarity:

> It is the necessity of the adhesion of *all* to a judgement as example of a universal rule that one cannot enunciate . . . Such would be the effect of openmouthedness provoked by a unique exemplar whose beauty must be recognized in a judgement (mouth open), without conceptual discourse, without enunciation of rules (mouth mute, breath cut, *parole soufflée*).
>
> (Derrida 1987b: 96; original emphases)

So perhaps it should not seem entirely paradoxical that this view of the value of the aesthetic as such has become generalised into something like a precept, or a repeatable procedure, in the emphasis within twentieth-century literary studies on the exemplary rather than the narrowly exemplificatory status of literary texts. The professional vocation of New Criticism, for example, became precisely to attend to the *haecceitas*, the unassimilable and untranslatable 'thisness' of the literary text, resisting the temptation to the 'heresy of paraphrase', as Cleanth Brooks calls it (Brooks 1968: 157–75).

Superficially, it might seem as though the theoretical turn in literary studies has brought about a move in another direction, towards general explanation rather than particular exemplification. This might itself be exemplified by the recent move away from the practice of 'practical criticism' in higher education, especially in first-year courses, to general courses in literary theory. If the pedagogic principle behind practical criticism is that the student can be fitted by arduous confrontation with particular texts for the encounter with other texts as well as language in general, the introductory theory course seems to be intended to provide a grounding in concepts rather than technique, acquainting the student with a general, exchangeable set of questions which will in principle be available in the discussion of all texts, rather than attempting to inculcate a general sensitivity to the irreducible particularity of such texts. This is a move from metonymy to metaphor. The mobile metonymic equivalence between incommensurable and *sui generis* forms of exemplarity gives way to the metaphoric exchangeability of exemplification. This is to describe not the ways in which these practices function in themselves, but rather their ideal forms and the idealised form of their contrast; for one would have to acknowledge that, in practice, practical criticism is not purely 'practical' at all, that its staged encounters with the exemplary and the unrepeatable are always ways of exemplifying approved forms of texts and reading.

Those who are irritated by the growing dominion of theory in English studies often regret this development as a move away from the authority of the particular to the dubious claims of generality, a claim which is then open to various counter-arguments about the ideological imbeddedness of all claims for particularity. It is true, as Edward Said has observed, that the resistance to theory has often taken the form of a resistance to generality in general, as we might say (Said 1983: 7). But it is also the case that much contemporary theory has inherited and reproduced the resistance to generality of the New Criticism. I would go as far as saying that it is in fact the orientation towards the exemplary which forms the real ground of convergence between the New Criticism and some forms of poststructuralist reading practice, rather than, as is more conventionally argued, their shared overestimation of textuality.

The work and influence of Foucault and Derrida are instructive examples here. Both of them provide immensely strong and exemplary readings of texts whose status as examples they continually put in question. In doing so, they suggest ways in which their acts of reading might, indeed should be, extended to and replicated in other areas and with respect to other topics. And yet both writers have proved very hard acts to 'follow', in Kant's sense. Derrida's work is characterised by breathtaking synecdochic bravado, which can take one example, such as jotting by Nietzsche about his umbrella, and unfurl from it the whole story of Western attitudes towards truth, language, meaning and style (Derrida 1979). But, quite as often, Derrida works in the mode of the exemplary, insisting on the absolute singularity of his subjects and issues and, infuriatingly for some, resisting being led prematurely into the programmatic. Time and again, Derrida has refused to define the deconstructive theory of which his work would be the exemplary practice, or to offer grounds for distinguishing between proper and improper examples of deconstruction. 'Deconstruction', he has declared, 'does not exist somewhere pure, proper, self-identical, outside of its inscriptions in conflictual and differentiated contexts; it "is" only what it does and what is done with it, there where it takes place' (Derrida 1990: 14). This kind of deconstructive practice is here offered not as adumbration or consummation of some less conditioned or ideal method, for its exemplary 'taking place' does not stand in the exemplificatory place of some ideal deconstruction *an sich*.

Indeed, the whole question of exemplification and exemplarity has been a recurrent theme throughout Derrida's readings of other texts; such that one critic has recently suggested that, in a sense, Derrida's work has 'never been concerned with anything *other* than exemplarity' (Harvey 1992: 193). In his reading of Freud's *Beyond the Pleasure Principle*, for instance, Derrida is fascinated by the various literary examples which Freud brings forward to evidence the death drive and repetition compulsion. Derrida argues that Freud's argument is not only evidenced by his examples but re-enacted in his use of the examples, just as the use to which Freud puts the *fort:da* game (drawing it into his text, apparently putting it aside, and then subsequently retrieving the episode for his argument) recapitulates the structure of the game itself. Derrida remarks particularly on Freud's use of Tasso's *Gerusalemme Liberata*. What is uncanny about this narrative, he argues, is not the fact that it provides examples of the uncanny recurrence and repetition compulsion that are Freud's concerns in *Beyond the Pleasure Principle* (the murder of the beloved disguised as a man, the return of the slain Clorinda in a ghostly voice), but a more fundamental anticipation by the example of the theory which it is used to exemplify:

> The recourse to the literary 'example' cannot simply be illustrative in *Beyond* . . ., no matter what Freud seems to say about it . . . 'Literary fiction', which this rhetoric would seek to contain in the imaginary, already watches over like a fairy or a demon, the structure of the *fort:da*, its scene of writing or of inheritance in dissemination . . . [W]hat is *'most* moving' . . . no matter what Freud states, and which is stated here before him in order to impose itself upon him, is the repetition (call it 'literary' if you will, a kind of fiction which in any event no longer derives

from the imaginary), of those *unheimlich* repetitions of repetitions.

(Derrida 1987a: 342–3)

This concern with Freud's use of examples prepares for Derrida's critique later in *The Post Card* of Lacan's use of literary examples, and especially of Poe's 'The purloined letter', in which he argues that, by turning the story of the endless wanderings of the letter into an emblem or exemplification of castration, Lacan neutralises the force of the example, refusing to allow it to play with and across his own discourse. Derrida regrets that, in Lacan's use of 'The purloined letter',

> Literary writing . . . is brought into an *illustrative* position: 'to illustrate' here meaning to read the general law in the example, to make clear the meaning of a law or of a truth, to bring them to light in striking or exemplary fashion. The text is in the service of the truth, and of a truth that is taught.
>
> (ibid.: 426; original emphasis)

This particular argument has of course generated a whole series of subsequent purloinings, in which the use of literature by psychoanalysis and psychoanalysis by literature for the purposes of exemplification of a 'truth that is taught' is agonistically played through (Muller and Richardson 1988). The question raised in this debate concerns what the use of exemplification itself exemplifies or instances. In his reading of Freud, Derrida is also meditating upon the ways in which *Beyond the Pleasure Principle* does and does not offer itself to him as an exemplification of a procedure or law; as such, he is simultaneously inspecting and suspecting the exemplary status of his own text, the method of his own non-methodical reading of their (non-)exemplarity. More recently, and perhaps of more direct relevance for the present discussion of the use of examples in literary criticism, Derrida has identified the effect of the literary with this very condition of exemplary undecidability:

> Something of literature will have begun when it is not possible to decide whether, when I speak of something, I am indeed speaking of something (of the thing itself, this one, for itself) or if I am giving an example, an example of

something or an example of the fact that I can speak of something, of my way of speaking of something, of the possibility of speaking in general of something in general.

(Derrida 1992: 33–4)

These remarks may suggest that the endlessly renewed demand for examples of the relation between deconstructive thought and literature, or examples of readings that demonstrate or bear out the value of deconstruction for the reading of literary texts, may be mistaken to the degree that it assumes and requires a regularity of the exemplificatory relation which it is precisely the character of 'literature' to resist. 'It is of this, and for this, that literature (among other things) is exemplary', Derrida continues; 'it always is, says, does something other, something other than itself, an itself which moreover is only that, something other than itself. For example or *par excellence*: philosophy' (ibid.: 35).

Given all of this, however, the great problem for deconstruction has not been its difficulty or its remoteness from practical instance so much as its success, the fact that, despite all of the elaborate precautions offered by Derrida, de Man and others, something that calls itself deconstructive practice has not only been institutionalised but has even become routine in some institutions. Readers, primers and exemplifications of deconstruction abound – I have perpetrated one myself and would do so again – with exemplification exerting on exemplarity all its force of regularisation.

Foucault's work is, if anything, even more beset by this contrast between the exemplificatory and the exemplary. Foucault's examination of the powers of institutionalised discourse has exemplified for many the possibility of an entirely new way of writing history and conceiving relations of power in language and culture. Foucault himself often spoke of the inaugural and exemplificatory character of his own work. But, at the same time, that work is driven by a desire to attend to the exemplary, to the force of what gets reduced by the force of institutional knowledge to the instrumental status of an example. Foucault's work offers the paradoxically unredeemable promise of a history of unassimilable singularities apart from or prior to and aside from their systematisation. The famous catalogue which Foucault quotes from Borges at the beginning of *The Order of Things* is just this kind of example of a series of exemplarities, which refuse the status of examples. The purgative laughter released by Borges' grotesque taxonomy depends upon our sense of being removed from the ordinariness of our orders of discourse, our sense of 'the stark impossibility of thinking *that*' (Foucault 1970: xv; original emphasis). This impossibility depends in large part upon the way in which the taxonomy instances and refuses the passage from example to exemplified, presenting a range of examples which seem simultaneously to saturate and exhaust the categories they exemplify. Unsurprisingly perhaps, given the difficulty of thinking systematically about what eludes systematic exemplification, Foucault's work has been most influential as a model of how the networks of power in discourse may be mapped and exemplified, rather than as an anticipation of the ways in which the fugitive powers of the exemplary in discourse might be registered, preserved and ramified.

Contemporary theory and, to the extent that they are now (if unevenly) dominated by contemporary theory, the academic institutions of literature in general are caught in particularly exquisite forms of the dilemma of exemplarity. Undeniably, such theory has brought about a huge and concerted refusal of the link between exemplary works and the category of literature, as the Kantian rule of ruleless singularity has been replaced by post-metanarrative notions of unassimilable difference or plurality. But the latter form of exemplarity can be and is being captured within the circuit of exemplification just as the earlier one could, and was. An example here might be Lyotard's reformulation of the Kantian exemplary as part of his assault on the authority of metanarratives. For Lyotard, the authentic work of the avant-garde is a putting into question of the norms and expectations of art itself. The singularity of the postmodern avant-garde consists in its search in a prospective 'future anterior' tense, for 'the rules of what *will have been done*' (Lyotard 1984: 81; original emphasis). The postmodern work cannot be said to exemplify any rule or category; interpreted in terms of the Kantian sublime, it provides, at most, a case of the failure of correspondence between case and category:

[The sublime] takes place . . . when the imagination fails

45

to present an object which might, if only in principle, come to match a concept. We have the Idea of the world (the totality of what is), but we do not have the capacity to show an example of it. We have the idea of the simple (that which cannot be broken down, or decomposed), but we cannot illustrate it with a sensible object which would be a 'case' of it.

(ibid.: 78)

In such a disposition, it proves necessary to respond to Wittgenstein's formula that the world is 'everything that is the case' (*alles, was der Fall ist*), by distinguishing phenomena which accord with our sense of what is the case from the indeterminate, exemplary 'event' which does not function as a case: 'the case is not that which is the case. The case is: *There is, It happens.* That is to say: *Is it happening?*' (Lyotard 1988: 79; original emphases). And, if art cannot be said to exemplify pre-existing rules, then the criticism and theory which concern themselves with the explication of that art cannot legitimately work with exemplification of rules either. But, of course, this notion, like the Kantian notion, can scarcely avoid becoming immensely productive of examples; and a work such as Thomas Docherty's *After Theory* (1990), which draws extensively on Lyotard's notion of the future anterior of the avant-garde case, is able skilfully to multiply examples of this particularly postmodern form of exemplary unprecedentedness.

A further instructive example of the irresistible force of the exemplificatory is to be found in one of the few essays to have considered the question of the example in contemporary theory (and, as such, it is an essay from which I have learned a great deal), H.W. Fawkner's 'The concept of taste: theory in the post-modernist era' (1990). Although Fawkner is more sensitive than most to the problems posed by the Kantian notion of the exemplary, his essay is instructively unable to avoid them in its own formulation. Fawkner's argument is that Kant's distinction between the conceptual and the aesthetic is broken down in postmodern theory (he instances Derrida's reading of Kant in *The Truth in Painting*). Oddly, perhaps, Fawkner chooses to exemplify this contemporary breakdown by means of Shakespeare's *Antony and Cleopatra*. In a fine study of the language, and especially the language of metaphor in that play, Fawkner shows how

Shakespeare resists and complicates the separation of example and generality on which Kant's notion of the aesthetic rests, and as such is a counter-example to that theory of exemplarity. It is not that Shakespeare is beyond the conceptual but that his language endlessly puts the relations between the conceptual and the non-conceptual into play:

> [I]nside the 'concrete' example (*Antony and Cleopatra*, Shakespeare), the 'abstract' (theory, law, conceptuality, thought, paradigm) is already opening up. The problematic can be formulated in post-structuralist terms: Can we separate the inside from the outside? Can we hold apart example and theory? What happens if the inside (example, work, text, material instance) is already 'larger' than the outside (canon, theory, ideality) that should enfold it?
>
> (Fawkner 1990: 101)

There is an interesting paradox at work in Fawkner's argument about the postmodern paradoxicality of the example. Fawkner resists the Kantian notion of the exemplariness of art by pointing to the ways in which Shakespeare interrogates the example in *Antony and Cleopatra*. But the result of this, despite Fawkner's demurrals on this question, is precisely to claim Shakespeare's work as exemplary in the Kantian sense – as governed, and governable, by no rule. It is governed by no rule because it resists the Kantian rule about works of art being governable by no external rules. It is therefore by resisting the prescription that works of art should be exemplary, rather than merely exemplificatory, that Shakespeare is brought successfully to exemplify that Kantian requirement of non-exemplification. In seeming to break the rule of rulelessness, the concept of non-conceptuality, the works of Shakespeare precisely instance that rule, embody that concept. The exemplificatory force of Shakespeare's exemplarity becomes even more emphatic because of his synecdochic status in Fawkner's essay: Shakespeare instantiates here not (as is more usual) the force of literature as such but the particular challenge of postmodern literature (and criticism).

I should like to make this particular example do some synecdochic work itself, for I think it exemplifies some of the characteristic problems which attach to the activity of exemplification in contemporary literary studies. In fact, the influence of literary theory in English has been neither simply to consolidate the claims of exemplarity on the one hand, nor simply to deepen the need for exemplification on the other, but rather to tighten and accelerate the circuit of exchange between the two. The more theory stresses the difficulty of the procedures of exemplification, the more pressure there is, within and outside theory, for exemplifications of that difficulty. The more, for instance, the category of 'English literature' is put into doubt, largely through examples of texts and objects of study which fail to exemplify Englishness or literariness, the more demand there is within the discipline of English literature for examples of work that show the practical consequences of abandoning the conception of English literature, or, in other words, for exemplifications of the collapse of the passage between example and exemplified.

Too often theory has attempted to escape the circuit of exemplification by simply intensifying the demand for exemplarity, in all of its currently acclaimed modes, such as nomadology, micrology and the other fetishisms of the particular that have recently been surveyed by Alan Liu (1990). But the inversive logic of the exemplary makes every assertion of its force an exemplification, and hence a compromising of that force. This is illustrated, I think, in the work of Gregory L. Ulmer, one of the very few theorists to have considered the issues of exemplarity for pedagogic practice in the light of deconstruction. In his *Applied Grammatology* (1985), Ulmer is concerned to rethink the metaphor that makes of the classroom the scene or stage in which a predetermined script is obediently acted out, and of education generally a process in which inherited forms of knowledge and value are passively, untransformatively exemplified (see my earlier discussion in Connor 1989: 138–9, 213–15). In his more recent book *Teletheory*, Ulmer focuses more closely on the practices of writing in educational institutions, urging the adoption of personalised, non-alphabetic forms of writing (such as writing in film and video), which would allow for what he calls 'euretic' processes of invention rather than hermeneutic processes of interpretation. Bravely, Ulmer provides his own example of what such writing might be like, a text entitled 'Derrida at the Little Bighorn', which cuts interestingly between his own curriculum vitae, a re-imagining of Custer's Last Stand and a meditation on the work of Derrida. This text comes at the end of a long and densely meditated argument about the need for and nature of the new pedagogy, which offers parallels and anticipations of the genre he calls 'mystory' in a number of case studies. Works like Wittgenstein's *Brown Book*, Barthes' *A Lover's Discourse*, Ponge's *The Making of the Pré*, Kelly's *Post-Partum Document* and Cage's *Mushroom Book* are offered as examples of a way to 'approach knowledge from the side of not knowing what it is, from the side of the one who is learning, not from that of the one who already knows' (Ulmer 1989: 106). Throughout, Ulmer recommends the mode of allegory over what he terms 'allegoresis', a distinction which corresponds to some degree to the distinction I have been discerning between exemplarity and exemplification. For Ulmer, allegoresis requires us to interpret an object or text in terms of what it stands for, while in allegory a text is not taken as an example or symptom of anything but itself, and so could constitute 'an original, native language, fully capable of doing the work of academic discourse as research and teaching' (ibid.: 20). The problem here is precisely that Ulmer prepares us so elaborately for the unprecedented in his own 'euretic' writing, instructing us carefully through all his examples in the nature of its spontaneity. As a result, in the very act of proclaiming its exemplary nature as prototype, 'Derrida at the Little Bighorn' becomes exemplification, allegoresis.

A more helpful reading of the rhetoric of the exemplary is offered in J. Hillis Miller's *The Ethics of Reading* (1987). Inevitably perhaps, Miller returns to the work of Kant, though not, as one might expect, to the third *Critique* but to the *Foundation of the Metaphysics of Morals* (Kant 1978). Here, he fixes on a certain inescapable contradiction within Kant's claim that the moral law, as a purely formal orientation towards universalisability, is to be distinguished rigorously from every actually existing example of law or code. This claim means that the moral law can never be directly embodied or exemplified. At the same time, however, precisely because the moral law cannot be exemplified, it will always be necessary to provide examples of it. If the moral law requires me never to act in such a way that the principles governing my actions could not be generalised to all human beings in the same situation, the only way in which I can effect this generalisation, says Miller, is by narrative, to which I must always resort in order to test whether my private act can indeed function as a universal example. In a brilliant analysis, Miller shows how Kant is forced to use an example to show how the moral law works – the example of someone who makes a promise, meaning to break it – which actually contradicts his principles. The point is that the structure of a promise is such that it always contains the possibility that the promise will not be kept. Arguing that it is an intrinsic feature of all language, and especially of performative language like that of promising, that its facts can exceed the intentions of its users, Miller shows how Kant's own promise to provide an example which will demonstrate the categorical necessity of keeping promises is undermined by his example of the unkept promise (Miller 1987: 36–7). This is not merely an accidental defect in Kant's argument, for Miller believes that it is impossible either to provide satisfactory exemplification of the moral law or to escape the need for such exemplification. Derrida has also observed the problematic status of examples in Kant; although Kant condemns examples as artificial aids ('*Gängelwagen*': 'wheelchairs') for those who lack the natural faculty of judgement, he cannot avoid them and the corruptions they bring:

> The exemplary wheelchairs are thus prostheses which replace nothing. But like all examples (*Beispielen*), as Hegel will have pointed out, they play, there is play in them, they give room to play. To the essence, beside the essence (*beiher*), Hegel goes on to make clear. Thus they can invert, unbalance, incline the natural movement into a parergonal movement, divert the energy of the *ergon*, introduce chance and the abyss into the necessity of the *Mutterwitz*.
> (Derrida 1987b: 79)

Of course, as Irene E. Harvey has demonstrated in her illuminating exploration of the thematics of exemplarity in Derrida's work, such an assertion of the intrinsically delinquent nature of the example can never wholly escape the desire for the law, and the form of its dominion exercised through the economy of exemplarity. Writing of Derrida's characterisation of the Holocaust in terms of Hegel's notion of God as the form of pure exemplarity, Harvey argues that

The Holocaust . . . is without essence, without law; it is the idiom again repeated here in its absolute form. In turn, it becomes an example of the non-example, and we have re-placed this non-essential instance, this unique uniqueness, back into an economy of exemplarity, indeed, the economy of exemplarity which is here as elsewhere isomorphic (if not identical in substance as well) with that of metaphysics.

(Harvey 1992: 201)

For Harvey the blind spot of Derrida's work is his dependence upon this economy of exemplarity, or, in my preferred terms, the recurrence of relations of exemplification within exemplarity. But I am not sure that this dependence is really such a blind spot in Derrida's work, or that his enquiries into the conditions of exemplification merely blindly presuppose without inspection the necessity of an economy of exemplarity. It may be that Harvey, like Ulmer, has a vision of an absolute escape from the necessity of exemplificatory relations (these being exemplary of dialectical thinking and metaphysics in general) which Derrida's work does not easily tolerate.

It seems to me that a paradoxical view of the example is one that would be more profitable to explore and inhabit than the polarised alternatives I have been discussing so far, namely, the institutionalising of theory in exemplification, and the allergic abstention from any kind of institutionalisation in the cult of exemplarity (as I have been trying to show, there is deep and usually unexamined collusion between the two polarities). In the view I am attracted to, exemplification is grasped as a certain kind of practical necessity for theory. For I do not think that this desire for exemplification is necessarily or uniformly a bad thing, and think we should forgo, as itself a kind of metaphysical wholehoggery, the denunciation of any reading or teaching practice which does not entirely escape the metaphysical economy of exemplification. Indeed, it would be hard for anyone who is a teacher as well as researcher to wish to abandon the responsibility for exemplification, since teaching consists very largely in facilitating the passage from the exemplary to the exemplificatory, in making it clear why the works of Derrida or Irigaray have a generalisable force in the lives of our students. But at the same time, we would do well not to underestimate the power of the humble example, along with all the relationships which hold it in place and which it holds in place itself, to intern and regularise inquiry and the institutional forms in which inquiry happens. Exemplification and the endless demand for exemplification in the modern university are sometimes uncomfortably difficult to disentangle from the more vulgarly palpable forms of the constraining of discourse, for instance the ways in which learning and education are being presently reconstructed as technological 'training'. No better, or worse, example of the brutal narrowing of critical thought into exemplification need be imagined than pathetic attempts in British universities currently to constitute the value of the humanities and critical social sciences in terms merely of the imparting of 'transferable skills', the requirement for the activity of reading texts for example to provide a series of exemplificatory simulations of the techniques of 'negotiating', 'communication', 'teamwork' and 'problem-solving' allegedly demanded by 'that thing obscurely and tranquilly named "real life" ' (Derrida 1990: 124).

I think that some of my examples show that we could profitably breach the simple binarism between the exemplary and the exemplificatory, and resist being governed by the alternatives that this binarism procures. This would mean resisting the utopian desire to kick out from the instrumentality of exemplification into the clear waters of absolute singularity, while also attempting to be aware of the constrictions of the desire for the example. This is more than a pragmatic counsel to avoid unbecoming extremes, for I think it might also be taken as embodying a principle: the principle that the regularising force of the example should always in principle be at stake, and that intellectual institutions and disciplines should exist not only to maintain the coherent syntax of relation between examples and what they exemplify, but also to focus and frame the questions which may disorder this syntax. What we need, in short, is not more examples of theory in practice, but an adversary theory of the practice of examples.

BIBLIOGRAPHY

Barthes, Roland (1983) *The Fashion System*, trans. Matthew Ward and Richard Howard, New York: Hill & Wang.

—— (1990) *The Pleasure of the Text*, trans. Richard Miller, Oxford: Basil Blackwell.

Brooks, Cleanth (1968) *The Well Wrought Urn: Studies in the Structure of Poetry*, 2nd edn, London: Dobson.

Connor, Steven (1989) *Postmodernist Culture: An Introduction to Theories of the Contemporary*, Oxford: Basil Blackwell.

Derrida, Jacques (1979) *Spurs: Nietzsche's Styles*, trans. Barbara Harlow, Chicago and London: University of Chicago Press.

—— (1987a) *The Post Card: From Socrates to Freud and Beyond*, trans. Alan Bass, Chicago and London: University of Chicago Press, 1987.

—— (1987b) *The Truth in Painting*, trans. Geoff Bennington and Ian Macleod, Chicago and London: University of Chicago Press.

—— (1990) 'Afterword: toward an ethic of discussion', trans. Samuel Weber, in Gerald Graff (ed.) *Limited Inc*, Evanston, Ill.: Northwestern University Press.

—— (1992) 'Passions: an oblique offering', trans. David Wood, in David Wood (ed.) *Derrida: A Critical Reader*, Oxford: Basil Blackwell.

Docherty, Thomas (1990) *After Theory: Postmodernism/Postmarxism*, London: Routledge.

Fawkner, H.W. (1990) 'The concept of taste: theory in the postmodernist era', in Danuta Zadworna-Fjellestad and Lennart Björk (eds) *Criticism in the Twilight Zone: Postmodern Perspectives on Literature and Politics*, Stockholm: Almqvist & Wiksell.

Foucault, Michel (1970) *The Order of Things: An Archaeology of the Human Sciences*, London: Tavistock Publications.

—— (1981) 'The order of discourse', trans. Ian Macleod, in Robert Young (ed.) *Untying the Text: A Post-Structuralist Reader*, London: Routledge & Kegan Paul.

Harvey, Irene E. (1992) 'Derrida and the issues of exemplarity', in David Wood (ed.) *Derrida: A Critical Reader*, Oxford: Basil Blackwell.

Kant, Immanuel (1978) *Foundation of the Metaphysics of Morals*, trans. Lewis White Beck, Indianapolis, Ind.: Bobbs-Merrill Educational Publishing.

—— (1988) *The Critique of Judgement*, trans. James Creed Meredith, Oxford: Clarendon Press.

Liu, Alan (1990) 'Local transcendence: cultural criticism, postmodernism, and the romanticism of detail', *Representations*, 32: 75–113.

Lyotard, Jean-François (1984) *The Postmodern Condition: A Report on Knowledge*, trans. Geoff Bennington and Brian Massumi, Manchester: Manchester University Press.

—— (1988) *The Differend: Phrases in Dispute*, trans. Georges van den Abbeele, Manchester: Manchester University Press.

Miller, J. Hillis (1987) *The Ethics of Reading: Kant, de Man, Eliot, Trollope, James, and Benjamin*, New York: Columbia University Press.

Muller, John P. and Richardson, Wiliam J. (eds) (1988) *The Purloined Poe: Lacan, Derrida, and Psychoanalytic Reading*, Baltimore, Md. and London: Johns Hopkins University Press.

Said, Edward (1983) 'Opponents, audiences, constituencies, and community', in W.J.T. Mitchell (ed.) *The Politics of Interpretation*, Chicago: University of Chicago Press.

Ulmer, Gregory L. (1985) *Applied Grammatology: Post(e)-Pedagogy from Jacques Derrida to Joseph Beuys*, Baltimore and London: Johns Hopkins University Press.

—— (1989) *Teletheory: Grammatology in the Age of Video*, New York and London: Routledge.

4

LEAVING PARTIES AND LEGACIES

Reflections across the binary divide on a decade of Englishes

Helen Taylor[1]

Theory has broken down the walls and let in the air. It has taken an English which was threatening to become preoccupied with endless monographs on Henry James and opened it up to issues of class, race, gender and popular culture in ways that have proved revolutionary and (in the polytechnics and colleges) productive of new courses and new integrations of subjects. Those of us who remember the well-wrought urns of 1950s criticism can't help but be glad that somebody cracked them.

(John Daniel, *PACE*, June 1991)

How do we define the 'crisis in English Studies?' Starved of resources, crushed by student numbers, concussed by subliterate managers, we no longer know what is worth teaching nor believe ourselves capable of teaching it.

(A polytechnic lecturer, letter to H.T., July 1991)

July 1990. Two versions of my leaving party.

The first, for a feminist whose career had taken her from a Leavisite and New Critical training in 'English' to a job in one of the young polytechnics. There, after early years of liberal studies horrors, she helped design a humanities degree course and after seventeen years, as a new MA in women's studies was about to get under way, she was off to a university post. At the party, she reflected on her years of growing up/older largely with the same group of people; on her personal intellectual growth, the department's massive course expansion and growth in student numbers, struggles against cuts, development of new subject areas and the recruitment of new kinds of

55

student – mature, non-standard entry, disabled, female, minority ethnic, etc. She had benefited from the support of her head of department and long-time colleagues, in research, teaching and administrative innovations. She was sad to leave behind a flourishing, lively department.

The second version. A woman joined the polytechnic at a time when her office had no female toilet; she had learned over the years how symbolically apt that omission had been. Her feminism had been at first subtly derided and undermined by senior male colleagues; her intellectual confidence zapped by sexual harassment, non-promotion and overwork. She had been saved by joining the Marxist-Feminist Literature Collective; relished the support of socialist-feminist academics outside her institution; and, fortunately for her, once-maligned feminist research became, through the 1970s and 1980s, much in demand from students and publishers. In the 1980s she had become profoundly depressed by Thatcherite attacks on education which never gave credit to the pile-'em-high mass education on the cheap, in which public sector HE teachers were obliged to be engaged, with precious few resources and derisory financial reward. She had tried to do her bit in the resource-led, market-dominated poly, recruiting lucrative American students and running short courses, but she was growing sick of the discourses of balance sheets and performance indicators. She was ready for a change; a university post might at least give her space to research, teach and write without calling upon her to be simultaneously a filing-clerk, counsellor and salesperson. 'Out from under the wire,' said the head of department. 'Lucky bugger,' muttered many others.

I offer two narratives, for they are both partly true. I felt, and still feel, ambiguous about leaving a 'cost-efficient' poly, as it then was, for a relatively financially stable university which offers the seductions of study leave, small classes, regularly cleaned windows and posh white stationery. Like most poly teachers, I've relished the shift in higher education from an elitist to a more democratic model which embraced so many students who always assumed their class, gender, education or race would exclude them from taking degrees; I also grew up in that culture of resistance which public sector education became under three Conservative governments. I was aware that the constant demands on poly and college teachers collaboratively to research, rethink, revise, renew courses and teaching methods had toughened me and given me a taste for collective work.

The last decade of my poly career was coloured by the 'crisis in English studies', and much of my intellectual energy had been focused on institutional struggles over the weighting of 'literary theory' and popular culture in course outlines. At my party, fragmented memories returned. My first tentative attempt to introduce a women's writing course into the English syllabus condemned by a senior male colleague ('I've been kicked around by women all my life and now they want their own courses'), and queried by a CNAA panel member ('Why *Women* and Literature? Why not – say – *Flowers* and . . .?'); Catherine Belsey giving a guest lecture on the negative influence of Leavis within English departments; the then head of English, himself once a student of Leavis, didn't attend, as he said he'd get 'too angry'. An argument in the late 1970s with a colleague when co-writing an article on our feminist course; she found the term 'literary production' crudely reductive and felt it allowed no space for creative genius. And then there were the students, many mature, with all their contradictory, irritating, surprising demands and needs to keep me intellectually alert and emotionally exhausted, but much-quoted by me and others to influence departmental organisational, pedagogic and theoretical developments. We may, for instance, have wished to ignore the 'crisis in English studies', but it had to be addressed by someone when students came along saying, 'What is this thing called structuralism, and who the hell is Colin MacCabe?'

My own intellectual progression towards an engagement with feminism and cultural materialism was urged on by students' political, academic and emotional requirements. Most dramatically, the pressure from mature women students (often fresh from WEA, university continuing education or Open University classes) hastened curriculum changes to include feminist theory, texts and democratic classroom practices. And our students' postmodern indifference to those jealously guarded subject definitions of and boundaries between English, women's studies and cultural studies enabled us to move from 'English' to 'Englishes', 'writing', 'texts' and 'literary studies', with popular fiction, multicultural concerns, world literature, film and reader-response easing into more central positions on the degree programme.

What I describe will be immediately recognisable to many former poly and college lecturers. I am part of a large and privileged group of forty-somethings who got their first academic posts shortly after the 1969 designation of polytechnics, with those new 'humanities' and 'literary and historical studies' schools/departments, the work of which we had the freedom to define and mould. We have grown middle-aged and experienced together, endlessly policed/harangued/monitored and evaluated by those initialled bodies (CNAA, NAB, CATE, PCFC, CATS, etc) which defined our institutional lives. We were the lucky ones, with permanent jobs through a period of very uneven growth in HE, including virtually the whole 1980s, which saw almost no junior lecturer appointments and which left a 'lost generation' of peripatetic part-time academics/ teachers (Pinkney 1990: 3–9). We had a fairly free rein to develop subject areas and to explore cross-disciplinary work and innovative teaching methods which students enjoyed and our employers recognised as marketable money-spinners. Increasingly, the student-consumers 'bought' social history, ecology, cultural and communication studies, women's studies and literary theory. They came to us rather than the more traditional universities because of those, and also because we avoided assessment by three-hour unseen exam in favour of mixed essays, projects and exams. In terms of literary studies, one of the contradictions of Thatcherism in tertiary education is the 1980s' flourishing of 'theory', that 'bugbear of the right . . . embraced from the beginning by Marxists, feminists and other dissidents', because it *sold* (Belsey 1990: 75). Philip O'Neill summarised the sea-change in consumer-led English studies when he described those 'colleagues who insisted on seeing *Wuthering Heights* in terms of the children of the calm and the children of the storm . . . finding themselves with empty classrooms' (O'Neill 1991: 10).

For it is 'theory' which has made all the difference – however one understands or defines it (and I use it loosely to describe that body of critical work which has drawn on post-Saussurean, Marxist and feminist thought since the late 1960s). Since the late 1970s that word, used variously in tones of reverence, awe, contempt and downright ignorance to mean anything from 'all poststructuralist thought' to 'loony Marxist-feminist rubbish', has dominated the humanities (especially literary and cultural studies) and divided academics along political and philosophical lines. And since the MacCabe controversy in 1981 (see Bergonzi 1990, especially chapter 2), 'theory' has been given flesh through an institutional shift in the paradigm of English studies, forcing reluctant English academics to display their hands and embrace particular ideological positions that bear a direct relationship to their teaching practice. Divisions among English teachers opened up – of generation, gender, class, region, political and religious beliefs (occasionally race, but there are very few black or Asian English lecturers in British HE – an exclusion which has become increasingly unacceptable). Revisionist texts and series poured from publishing houses, many committed to locating the new theoretical developments in interdisciplinary pedagogic practice (in all sectors of education): series such as the Methuen, later Routledge, New Accents; Harper Collins' Cultural Studies Birmingham, Reading Popular Fiction; Routledge's English Texts, Thinking Gender; Virago's Education Series, Longman's Modern Women Writers; titles such as *Re-reading English, Rewriting English, Broadening the Context, Dialogue and Difference, Futures for English* (Widdowson 1982, Batsleer 1985, Green 1987, Brooker and Humm 1989, MacCabe 1988). More significant, perhaps, in terms of informal networking and collective collaboration were the stream of Birmingham Cultural Studies stencilled papers (now published by Harper Collins, as above), *Literature Teaching Politics Journal* (1982–7), *English in Education, English Magazine, NETWORK Newsletter, News from Nowhere, Magazine of Cultural Studies*, and the Council for University English (CUE) and Standing Conference of English in Polytechnic and College Higher Education (SCEPCHE) Newsletters. In line with the often bitter conflicts engendered by all this heady stuff, a great deal of the rhetoric surrounding the revision or rebirth of 'English' used militaristic imagery – of 'struck and endangered Fortress English' (Brooker 1987: 23); 'firing' and 'bursting' the canon (for instance, Bergonzi 1990); 'explosion' of new ideas and writing, even 'melt-down at the core of an academic discipline' (Widdowson 1990: 1221). 'Crisis' was seen to result in a 'revolution', which 'toppl[ed] the English citadel' (*Daily Telegraph* on the Ruskin Conference, 20 June 1991); 'battle lines' were always being drawn (usually at Oxford University, according to the press, though they should have come to Bristol Poly, as it was then . . .) It livened things up for Left English teachers, seeing ourselves embattled against both Thatcher's governments and our anti-theoretical colleagues. Our working and intellectual lives could be dramatised as struggle, and while few claimed that revolution would occur as a direct result of the English seminar, there was an exhilarating sense of real shifts of power and intellectual influence which were having repercussions beyond the academy.

A SORT OF REVOLUTION

And indeed, a revolution of sorts has occurred. Look, for instance, at what happened to the academics who set up Literature Teaching Politics in the early 1980s, whose New Accents and other theoretical works berated the complacent conservatism of the academy. As with other revolutions, some of them have replaced the old guard; after a spate of early retirements induced by university cuts in the early 1980s, vacancies at senior level were filled by visibly active staff – many of whom had defined themselves as politically in opposition to the establishment which now invited them in. Although the polytechnics only instituted professorships shortly before gaining university status (and actively publishing poly teachers tended to avoid very senior positions entailing heavy administrative duties), recent chairs reflect a political, and indeed a gender, shift: at the older universities, people such as John Barrell (Sussex), Catherine Belsey, Terence Hawkes and Christopher Norris (Cardiff), Simon Frith (Strathclyde), Nicole Ward Jouve (York), Lisa Jardine and Jacqueline Rose (Queen Mary and Westfield, London), Janet Todd (University of East Anglia); at the newly designated universities, Antony Easthope (Manchester Metropolitan), Sandra Harris (Nottingham Trent), Frances Mannsakker (Glamorgan), Peter Widdowson (Middlesex) and the late Raman Selden (Sunderland). Other key Left figures are now in (university) readerships and senior lectureships and (new university) principal lectureships, with yards of series editorships and journal editorial board credits to their names. The influence of all these may be seen in the many MA programmes in critical theory, women's studies and gay studies which now exist alongside expanding cultural studies undergraduate and graduate work. In the late 1980s and early 1990s, the gaps their promotions have left, as well as new openings created by a huge increase of student numbers, have seen adverts requiring staff to teach literary theory, women's writing, perhaps a little cultural studies or film on the side. Tony Pinkney suggests, 'To be a 27 year-old woman now, intellectually engaged in some way or other in the field of women's writing, is to have reached the age of employability' (Pinkney 1990: 4), and it is true that such a woman – who only a few years earlier would have invited academic marginality, endless part-time contracts and much head-shaking from senior male management – is enjoying some success. This young hopeful must, however, be seen in the context of a huge pool of (largely female, no longer 27) long-serving part-timers who stand little chance of gaining a permanent appointment.

For the establishment press, the most significant of the promotions so far (1993) has been the elevation of Terry Eagleton to Warton Professorship of English Literature at Oxford University. In the first half of 1991, 'Red Tel' (as the *Observer* dubbed him) seemed rarely off the review pages. 'Oxford gets a Marxist', proclaimed the *Observer* (21 April 1991), while the *Guardian* (15 August 1991) published a hostile interview of Eagleton by Catherine Bennett. Referring sardonically to Eagleton's apparently reiterated self-description as 'the Barbarian within the Citadel', Bennett quoted Valentine Cunningham's comment that 'he's been here so bloody long that he *is* the citadel' and she asked how he was 'helping the downtrodden from his sofa in the citadel'. In an earlier piece, a review of his book *Ideology*, James Wood mocked the Eagleton of radical slogans now seated at the high table: 'After the Marxist meals come the bourgeois banquets, after the long knives come the fish knives' (*Guardian*, 23 May 1991). Eagleton is easily parodied, and his apparent insularity from other British HE institutions does lead him to claims and critiques about English studies which sound positively quaint to those who long since abandoned compulsory Anglo-Saxon and notions of 'the English canon'. However, for many hard-pressed teachers of English his work has been immensely important, struggling as so many had to with inaccessible theorists which Eagleton made coherent and relevant. Helen Carr (*Observer*, 14 July 1991) speaks for many when she argues that he 'has done more than anyone to bring insular and anti-intellectual British literary studies into contact with European intellectual life', while Sally Ledger, an undergraduate on an unreconstructed English course as late as 1982–5, says that after reading his *Literary Theory*, ' "English" suddenly seemed like a controversial, dynamic and exciting field of study rather than a static body of texts. It was exhilarating, too, to discover that there was space for my politics in "English" studies.' It is a testimony to Eagleton's ability to bring continental theories to life that the book Ledger cites has sold over 100,000 copies. His chair is a significant triumph for the new Englishes in British higher education.

And, helped by books such as his, greater staff confidence and the influence of reader-response-inspired criticism, HE English teachers have found a variety of ways of introducing literary theory into the classroom. Two examples will illustrate this. First, Aberystwyth University's new two-year introductory English course, 'Reading Theory/Reading Texts' is described thus:

> [I]f theory is to be taught, it has to be taught through a gradualist approach and in a way that attempts to demonstrate relevance to literary analysis. In the first year, we intend to investigate how and why we arrive at the readings we do; and we hope that students will begin to define critical positions of their own as a relatively self-aware process . . . The first year of the course emphasises skills and methods, the second year introduces recent literary theories and tendencies, covering narratology, marxist criticism, cultural materialism, feminism, psychoanalysis and post-structuralism . . . Students will appreciate that there has been debate about literature for as long as there has been literature; they will understand some of the terms in which it has been conducted, and they will see some of the strategies and positions behind its most recent phase.

At the University of East London, Maggie Humm teaches women's studies theory in terms of debates: 'Walker versus Spacks or Lorde versus Daly or Barrett versus Chicago. We also read fiction as theory i.e. Walker's *The Temple of my Familiar*, and theory as fiction i.e. Cixous.' Many English/literary studies teachers have stopped anguishing over dreary questions of the canon and what a student 'ought' to have read in three years. This is, of course, bolstered by the existence of new case studies employing different 'approaches', collections of essays and anthologies which juxtapose canonical with non-canonical works and query or contextualise the status of 'major' figures (see, for example, Newton and Rosenfelt 1985, Kaplan 1986, Widdowson 1989, *The Heath Anthology* 1990).

COLLECTIVITY AND COLLABORATION

This new confidence of the last decade or so has also grown through collective groups organised around pedagogy, publication and networking. Although they have tended to come and go, the following (which I list in random order) have had considerable impact on the progress of 'Englishes': NATE, The National Association for the Teaching of English (with publications, conferences and local groups for school teachers); NETWORK (for women in HE English, producing a regular newsletter and register of members); OEL, Oxford English Limited (which ran conferences, produced publications and helped put new options on women's writing and critical theory on the Oxford English syllabus); the Marxist-Feminist Literature Collective (which met for a few years and wrote a collective paper); LTP, Literature Teaching Politics (of which more later); ACS, The Association of Cultural Studies (which produced the journal *MOCS* and runs an annual conference and newsletter); HETE, Higher Education Teachers of English (an annual conference); ATCAL, Association for the Teaching of African, Caribbean and Associated Literatures; DUET, Developments in University English Teaching; CUE and SCEPCHE (both run conferences as well as newsletters); and the early 1990s attempt to develop a European-style Modern Languages Association, ESSE, European Society for the Study of English. All of these suffer(ed) from small resources and unpaid labour; Michael Green points to the unstable nature of such low-profile groupings when he says, 'It seemed possible at one stage to imagine three separate but often converging networks/magazines/dayschools in the adjacent areas of English Studies, Cultural Studies and Media Studies' (Green

1990: 34). He notes the demise of *Initiatives*, some of the BFI's secondary-school work, and LTP.

Of all those groups, LTP had most impact on me and, like Michael Green, I much regret its disappearance. Established in 1979 as a network of radical work in English studies, the aim of which was 'to analyse the plurality of relations between literature, teaching and politics, as a basis for change', LTP became an energetic, significant grouping until its last journal (1987) was published just as the eighth conference was cancelled for lack of support. The regional groups, six journals, seven conferences and one set of conference papers have all become important reference points; debates such as those on masculinity and *The Color Purple* have been reproduced and are now quoted on student exam answers. The early conferences were engaged in struggles against Thatcher's attacks on all sectors of education, at the same time as discussions of the dismantling of 'English', the relationships between literary and cultural studies, socialism and feminism, interdisciplinary and inter-institutional contacts, connections between writing, politics and reading in relation to community arts and the media, and rethinking the social relations of reading and writing. Conferences, held first at universities, then at the former polys and colleges, adopted workshop discussion and collective papers rather than star turns; they attracted general readers, community workers, students and writers as well as professional academics. As Jonathan Dollimore and Alan Sinfield said,

> Before LTP, teachers were political in the union, feminist groups or whatever; but to politicise your teaching, for many of us, seemed somehow improper . . . LTP afforded both the language and the confidence to 'come out' specifically in teaching as a socialist/feminist/gay/ unilateralist.
>
> (Taylor 1987: 12)

But the late 1980s were politically too difficult for everyone. Cuts, cuts and more cuts, heavier workloads, rock-bottom morale, the hopeless depression which overcame so many of us in Thatcher's last years, all took energy and time away. The publishers who flocked to the early conferences persuaded the most vocal academics to produce socialist-feminist monographs and essay collections, and there just wasn't the will to sustain communication across all educational sectors. Bristol produced the final LTP journal; despite making a profit through mail orders, we still have piles of copies in boxes. And yet, LTP achieved its aim of establishing literature as a political subject within and beyond the academy, and (in Michael Green's words) it 'marked out a space and a constituency perhaps even better than could originally have been hoped'. The exchange of ideas, course outlines, external examiners and so on has proved invaluable as informal networking and support; the rash of excellent collections on radical teaching and research, written by teachers in schools and in adult and further as well as higher education, owe much to its collective, cross-sector inspiration.

SCHOOLS ENGLISH

While celebrating the impact of new theoretical ideas, publications and groupings from the late 1970s to the early 1990s, it is important to mention the impact on schools (although with the complex debates going on at present about the national curriculum and 'A' level English, this will inevitably be sketchy). Schoolteachers influenced by the theoretical developments of recent years have produced dramatic changes in syllabus and teaching method; for instance, a typical English Literature 'A' level AEB 660 coursework folder might include texts that reflect an awareness of the class, race and gender spectrum of writers and their readers – *Oranges are not the Only Fruit, One Flew over the Cuckoo's Nest, Heat and Dust, Shirley Valentine*, Seamus Heaney's poetry – with a varied assessment pattern from a written exam of practical criticism through coursework consisting of short essays, a 3,000-word extended essay and play reviews. Oral presentation is also part of the assessment pattern in the national curriculum and at GCSE (a model many former polytechnics are now emulating). English teachers have successfully introduced more thorough historical and literary contextualisation, as well as encouraging the 'individual voice'. The growth of creative/personal writing in the English classroom as a way of understanding texts and exploring the dynamics of reader-response has produced a freer relationship between text and reader than is usually allowed in the HE seminar.

Ironically, school English teachers have been attacked from all sides. The Right sees progressive English as dangerously 'sociological' and a derogation of teachers' duty to instil 'standards' – that is, good spelling and grammar (note the Conservative government's suppression of the 1991 Language in the National Curriculum report); while the Left sees it as sloppy, 'Leavisite', inadequately theorised and historicised. At a Ruskin College conference, Professors Martin Dodsworth and John Barrell (from different political perspectives) both complained of first-year undergraduates' inability to read poetry and of their tendency to discuss characters in novels as if they were members of their families (see History Workshop 1991).

Rarely are English teachers given the credit due for the increasing numbers of English and cultural studies applications to colleges and universities, as well as the radical rethinking of examination and assessment modes. Accepting the English lesson as the one clear curriculum space in which students' emotional, intellectual and political experiences, questions and doubts may be explored through those imaginative responses university lecturers are nervous about, schoolteachers have continually experimented with ways of contextualising both language and literature. Besides, teachers' assimilation of cultural studies texts and concerns into that space (through a recognition of the centrality in children's lives of television, popular music, etc.) has led to a loosening of the distinctions between the two areas and produced a market for cultural studies degree courses, publications and new research. No wonder there was a sharp collective intake of breath at the July 1991 Ruskin Conference when Terry Eagleton – challenged to explain why his talk made no reference to television – said that he felt it had a merely negative influence on people, 'tying them down at home', and was thus out of his remit as a literary critic.

Speaking at the same conference, Jane Miller gave a powerful defence of the expansion in English and the role of English teachers in that – ironically, during a decade of cuts, mandatory testing, heavy pressures on teachers' time, energy and pay packets. Responding to the criticisms about 'standards' of English teaching and the decline of English culture, from Left, Right and Prince Charles, she claimed:

It needs to be said again and again. There are more not less of all these things: more reading, more literature, more writing, more Shakespeare. More children watching performances of Shakespeare and more taking part in them. Shakespeare, after all – new editions, videos, films, skits, parodies, misquotations and all – is big business. The texts themselves, as well as what they've come to stand for, are firmly on the syllabus.

(Miller 1991, unpublished paper: 2)

Referring also to the contemporary multicultural classroom, and the urgent need of all educators to respond to cultural/ linguistic diversity and difference, she said:

English teaching has faced up to cultural contradictions, to the migrations of a post imperialist world, to what Stephen Spender has quite rightly called the 'terrifying' thought of new writing by black and working-class writers; indeed to the modern world. All this has gone on in schools with virtually no support from academics . . . they've by and large distanced themselves fastidiously or concerned themselves only with those aspects of provision which affect the small proportion of school leavers they actually meet.

(ibid.: 3)

Susheila Nasta remarked on the scandalous record of British universities and former polys in developing multicultural, antiracist policies, by comparison with schools. The University of East London, one of the few universities with an honourable tradition here, has a student body approximately half of whom are not WASP males. Maggie Humm argues that these new cohorts of students, particularly Afro-Caribbeans, 'have large questions to ask. These cannot be addressed by chronological or even genre runthroughs of English literature, but require an understanding of economics/representation in the Third World.' UEL has responded to these demands by converting 'English' into cultural studies/media studies/women's studies, 'in other words area studies shed of racist/nationalist signifiers', as Humm puts it. Several other former polytechnic 'English' departments or schools are now called 'literary studies', 'literary and cultural studies', etc. In relation to the expansion of HE and the buoyant role of the humanities in attracting those groups hitherto excluded, as well as the opening up of new relationships with Western and Eastern Europe, the anxieties of university teachers over poor grammar (something revealed more clearly in wordprocessed than handwritten essays), and over the shift of emphasis in GCSE syllabi from Chaucer to Derek Walcott, Jane Austen to Jeanette Winterson (as if to 'set' one were to damn the other to extinction), seemed laughably parochial. Oxford University's debate over whether or not to drop compulsory Anglo-Saxon and Middle English ('The Beowulf battlers': *Guardian* 19 July 1991) looked grotesquely ethnocentric and anachronistic.

FEMINIST CRITICISM

Certainly, for me and for a large majority of the thirty-four academics I canvassed on the subject, the most significant theoretical and pedagogical development of the last decade has been feminist literary and cultural criticism. And despite the popular image of feminist critics as humourless, stern career-ists (*Nice Work*'s Robyn Penrose, *Possession*'s Maud Bailey, for instance), they have made and are still making much of the intellectual running in most institutions. This is all the more remarkable because women, who are by no means all interested in feminism, have been in a minority in (dare I say all?) English/ humanities departments and, as my own experience testifies, have faced often uninformed and emotional opposition to feminist curriculum innovations. From staff, that is. For the – largely female – student-led enthusiasm for women's studies work in all subject areas has forced departments slowly, often grudgingly, to transform their practices of pedagogy, appoint-ment and promotion. The employable 27-year-old Tony Pinkney describes is in demand only because her sisters before her took on a recalcitrant, sexist academy and insisted on altering gender (and, in some cases, race) imbalances. The formation of feminist studies through the women's movement of the 1960s and 1970s has meant that criticism is informed by an emphasis on the personal, sexual and domestic as political, with a practice that is collective and collaborative. Feminist English teachers have networked formally and informally, increasingly internationally and through databases; feminist consciousness-raising and self-help therapy practices have all helped subvert classroom, staffroom and conference procedures.

Given the recognised impact of feminist criticism, why is it that so many feminist academics are still waiting for recognition of their work in terms of promotion and appointment to key national bodies and institutions? A number of significant female theorists have left British higher education in disgust or despair; those few of us in senior posts are weary of being invited on to all key committees ('Of course we're not asking you as the token woman . . .'); and there are far too many women who have devoted themselves to teaching, counselling and nurturing students, passed over for promotion because they are 'inadequately published'. Feminist literary and cultural criticism has reached the stage at which it should be commanding its own chairs, departments and research centres; I suspect that it will remain a topic taught in humanities departments mainly by enthusiastic, young, over-burdened teachers who – in the current harsh climate – will eventually take their credentials and publications off to more comfortable, lucrative posts in Europe and the States.

THE FUTURE OF ENGLISHES?

I began with two versions of a leaving party, and much of this chapter has looked back with ambiguity to record a revolution in 'English' within HE. Certainly, despite conservative forces within and without English/literary studies departments, the subject has been revivified and revolutionised – most spectacularly by former polytechnics and colleges, and through radical criticism and teaching styles. English is now a series of 'Englishes', drawing on and contributing to literary theory, cultural studies, cultural materialism, discourse analysis, anti-racist theories, creative writing, as well as a host of other interdisciplinary areas (including now some science). It has been transformed by the pressure of new continental and Anglo-American theories and scholarship, and in creative response to constant demands from CNAA, HMI, etc., etc., and the increasing competition between institutions and sectors for students as fund-bearers. The year 1991 saw the first conference of ESSE; European schemes such as ERASMUS and

TEMPUS are having an impact on staff and student intellectual interests and priorities, and the new expanding Europe may well alter irrevocably everyone's academic and personal horizons. The media and cultural studies boom in schools is filtering through to higher education, where this established, expanding subject area may well attract away good students who hitherto applied for English courses (a trend Bernard Bergonzi notes, suggesting this should be appropriated by the social sciences, leaving English departments to focus on poetry and aesthetic concerns [Bergonzi 1990]). The end of the binary divide may forge productive, less defensive links between universities and the new polyversities, stirring up old university English departments to develop livelier courses and teaching methods to preserve their market share. The large number of retirements in my generation of academics during the next couple of decades will open the way for young, theoretically sophisticated teachers – many of them with cross-disciplinary first degrees and defining themselves as post-Marxist/feminist/structuralist/modernist. And the more collaborative mood indicated by 1991's mixed school and higher education conferences on English, focused on syllabus changes and united against governmental intervention, seems to suggest a lowering of barriers between the sectors.

Well, yes. This is a possible, optimistic scenario. But, as with my leaving party, there are negative indications and spectres at the feast. For the current government's intervention in schools English, supported and strengthened by reactionary educationists' and media comment including ominous attacks speeding across the Atlantic on 'political correctness' (PC), may well drive out innovations in English from *all* sectors. Higher education may be forced to share with schools a reactionary curriculum aimed at preserving our national culture, that is, more set texts by dead white Englishmen, and rewarding students for perfect spelling and no prepositions at the end of sentences. Students will continue to have views on curriculum change, but how are academics to listen to them when absurdly high staff–student ratios make informal human contact a rare luxury and exploratory seminar teaching gives way to large lectures with video repeats? And literary and cultural studies may be officially encouraged while the market is there, but what if low grants and crippling loans drive students into more immediately vocational areas? Furthermore, it has been hard to welcome the end of the binary divide when most academics (to judge from the overwhelming views of my sample) saw this as nothing more than a cost-cutting exercise to reduce university funding to the level of former colleges and polytechnics – with a few top universities allowed to continue humanities research, leaving the rest to get on with churning out graduates (preferably in two rather than three years). And because of the desperate scramble to be one of the chosen few, some universities have urged staff to drop plans for conferences, co-written and -edited books, and get on with the most seriously rated job (because it bumps up departmental research ratings): publishing individual monographs. The collaborative groups, networks and multi-authored collections which have given such zest to the English of the last twenty years, are now suffering badly from lack of funds, institutional commitment and individuals' time and energy.

We badly need those groups to secure the survival of the new literary and cultural studies, whose status is by no means secure. I cite two examples. Popular literature study is constantly under attack on prominent platforms and in the popular press despite, or because of, its growing popularity in schools (see the shock-horror greeting London University Examination Board's adoption of *The Day of the Jackal* as an 'A' level set text). And the Fulbright Commission's 1991 pamphlet on 'The future of American studies in the United Kingdom', apparently ignoring decades of serious cultural studies work in the USA and Britain, deplores as 'disastrous' the 'constant bombardment of the British public by American imagery projected through film and television and the popular press', and calls for 'an accepted list of British American Studies "experts" ' to instil 'a proper appreciation of the *real nature* of the United States' (emphasis added). It was also depressing to read, in relation to Sussex University's new MA programme focusing on gay and lesbian issues, 'Sexual dissidence and cultural change', not only the inevitable tabloid smears ('[Sussex] should be shut down and disinfected', Terry Dicks MP, *Daily Mirror*, 25 February 1991; 'I wonder if there is an oral, as well as a written exam', Richard Littlejohn, *Sun*, 28 February 1991), but also the genteelly homophobic tones of liberal Cambridge Professor Marilyn Butler, quoted in the *Observer* (31 March 1991) as worrying about its possible 'narrowness' and the fact that it could be 'something of a closed shop'. One academic described to me the wonderful research on lesbian writing being done by her PhD students, but also her anxiety about the cold climate affecting their future applications for grants, research and teaching posts. As with the early days of feminist criticism, there is still powerful institutional resistance to new theoretical and empirical developments in English(es), and plenty of opportunity for innovatory work to be strangled at birth.

CODA

I finished this article on a day when one of my ex-colleagues died of a massive stroke suffered at the Polytechnic, as it then was. He was 42, with three children under 10, and like others was facing another academic year of huge classes, new courses and commitments, library shortages and all the hassles of daily life in higher education today. I'm not saying the job killed him, though some will argue this and will reflect soberly on their own hard middle ages, with gross lack of time, leisure and pleasure. I do know that the burden on teachers in schools, colleges and universities gets heavier all the time – and there is less space for the creative, ruminative, well-researched thought which is essential to educational innovation and excitement. The last decade has seen the deaths of significant theorists and teachers of the calibre of Claire Johnston, Raman Selden, Allon White and Raymond Williams; many more teacher-writers have suffered physically, emotionally and financially the results of massive overwork, demoralisation and the anxieties of being part of a profession which is constantly under-resourced and under attack. The very qualities in English and all the humanities which have brought students flocking – imaginative teaching, discursive seminars, personal attention to oral and written work – cannot be sustained in a continental-style model of mass education. 'The state of theory' in British higher education is no theoretical problem. Regardless of the governing political party, alas, its future will be determined by those all too mundane problems of bums on seats, sizes of classrooms, market forces and performance indicators. Bright young researchers may think again before entering a profession which they see might suck them dry.

However, during the summer of 1991 I had a series of phone calls with members of the now defunct Bristol LTP group. Our LTP bank account still held £200 journal profits, awaiting a day when the group might revive and need funds. One of our members, then teaching at Exeter University, asked if we'd consider funding speakers for an international conference, 'Feminist criticism in the nineties', focusing on the legacy of Mary Wollstonecraft, whose *Vindication of the Rights of Woman* celebrated its bicentenary in 1992. This conference, like so many 'Into the Nineties' debates currently taking place, examined a variety of literary and cultural issues: feminism and literary history, difference, pedagogy, violence, consumption and reproduction. We all agreed to clear out the bank account and send it to Exeter. And though hating to admit the demise of LTP, I welcome this kind of legacy. Yet another academic conference may not be quite the heritage some of us had envisaged as a socialist-feminist educational future, but in the face of the 1980s attacks on 'English' and humanities teachers of all sectors, as well as the ominous growth of 'PC' charges in the early 1990s, it had to do.

NOTES

1 In order to prepare this chapter, I canvassed the views of many academics, of whom thirty-four replied to my questionnaire. Their ideas and information have informed this article, and I quote from their responses. While I am unable to do justice to their detailed, incisive and witty responses, I am extremely grateful to the following: Margaret Beetham, Bernard Bergonzi, John Bowen, Roger Bromley, Peter Brooker, Carolyn Brown, Charlotte Brunsdon, John Daniel, Helen Dennis, Jonathan Dollimore, John Drakakis, John Fletcher, Gill Frith, Simon Frith, Kate Fullbrook, Ed Gallafent, Marion Glastonbury, Michael Green, Maggie Humm, Vicki Joyce, Sally Ledger, Paddy Lyons, Peter Middleton, Jane Miller, Paulina Palmer, Lynne Pearce, Jim Porteous, Lyn Pykett, Marie Roberts, Anne Samson, Alan Sinfield, Carolyn Steedman, Duncan Webster and John Williams. I am also very grateful to Kate Fullbrook, Sally Ledger, Jim Porteous and Derrick Price for commenting so helpfully on an early draft.

BIBLIOGRAPHY

Batsleer, J., Davies, T., O'Rourke, R. and Weedon, C. (eds) (1985) *Rewriting English: Cultural Politics of Gender and Class*, London: Methuen.

Belsey, C. (1990) 'Theory in Cardiff', *News from Nowhere* 8, 75–80.

Bergonzi, Bernard (1990) *Exploding English: Criticism, Theory, Culture*, Oxford: Clarendon.

Brooker, P. (1987) 'Why Brecht, or, is there English after cultural studies?', in M. Green (ed.) *Broadening the Context*, London: John Murray.

Brooker, P. and Humm, P. (eds) (1989) *Dialogue and Difference: English into the Nineties*, London: Routledge.

Eagleton, T. (1983) *Literary Theory*, Oxford: Basil Blackwell.

The Fulbright Commission (1991) 'The Future of American Studies in the United Kingdom'.

Green, M. (1990) ' "Cultural Studies!" said the Magistrate', *News from Nowhere* 8: 28–37.

The Heath Anthology of American Literature (1990), Lexington, Mass. and Toronto: D.C. Heath.

History Workshop (1991) *History, The Nation and The Schools 3: The Future of English*, Oxford: Ruskin College.

Kaplan, C. (1986) *Sea Changes: Culture and Feminism*, London: Verso.

MacCabe, C. (1988) *Futures for English*, Manchester: Manchester University Press.

Miller, J. (1991) 'The future of English', paper given at Ruskin Conference, 'The future of English', June 1991.

Newton, J. and Rosenfelt, D. (eds) (1985) *Feminist Criticism and Social Change*, London: Methuen.

O'Neill, P. (1991) 'In defence of theory', *PACE* (SCEPCHE Newsletter), 3, 9–11.

Pinkney, T. (1990) 'Editorial: thirty-something', *News from Nowhere*, 8, 3–9.

Taylor, H. (1987) ' "Are we talking about literature?" A history of LTP', *Literature Teaching Politics Journal*, 6, 7–12 (available from H. Taylor, Dept of English, University of Warwick, Coventry CV4 7AL).

Widdowson, P. (ed.) (1982) *Re-Reading English*, London: Methuen.

—— (1989) *Hardy in History: A Study in Literary Sociology*, London: Routledge.

—— (1990) 'W(h)ither "English"?' in M. Coyle, P. Garside, M. Kelsall, J. Peck (eds) *Encyclopedia of Literature and Criticism*, London: Routledge.

5

TOWARDS A GOTHIC CRITICISM

Tony Pinkney

At the back of my house in Lancaster is a quiet street called Binyon Road. Off it runs an even sleepier cul-de-sac called Binyon Court. So silent and out of the way are these streets, so much of a miniature Land that Time Forgot, that they were the obvious place, a year or so ago, to take the stabilisers off my son's bicycle and teach him to ride it as a two-wheeler. One cluster of houses in Binyon Road is known, for postal purposes, as Laurence Court.

A 10-minute walk into Lancaster town centre explains this nomenclature. Set into the wall of the first house in the old High Street is a stone which announces:

Laurence Binyon
Poet *and* Scholar
1869–1943
Was Born at No. 1 High Street
On 10th August 1869

Binyon is, in fact, Lancaster's literary glory, our only home-grown poet and certainly the only entry under the heading 'Lancaster' in my edition of *The Oxford Literary Guide to the British Isles*. The italics – Poet *and* Scholar – in his commemorative stone are important. One could hardly say that Binyon's poetry remains a living force. Only one poem – 'For the Fallen' (1914) – remains current and even that is as often as not reduced, on war memorials and elsewhere, to its single most poignant line: 'They shall not grow old, as we that are left grow old.' I recall the line vividly enough from morning assembly at the grammar school I attended, where it appeared in gold leaf under the list of old boys who had been killed in the First and Second World Wars.

Yet as a 'scholar' Binyon is still in some ways a current figure. In 1991 I took a party of students on our modernism course to an exhibition on 'Dynamism: the art of modern life before the Great War' at the Liverpool Tate Gallery. In the exhibition catalogue, tucked away among glossy reproductions of aggressive Futurist and Vorticist paintings and sculptures, Lancaster's chief literary glory makes a surprise appearance:

> Besides Hulme, the other critics in London who assisted in the development of a new style [included] Laurence Binyon, poet and art historian, who took charge of the oriental prints and drawings department at the British Museum in 1913. By that date he had already written *Painting in the Far East*, in 1908 and *The Flight of the Dragon*, a book 'on the theory and practice of art in China and Japan', in 1911. Binyon was largely responsible for fostering an interest in the rhythms of a composition.
>
> (Curtis 1991: 32)

Poet *and* art historian again, we note – though in fact only Binyon's scholarship matters here. In the Leavisite account of British modernism, centred above all on T.S. Eliot and D.H. Lawrence, which dominated English studies for so long, Binyon is clearly a negligible figure; the more recent critical preference for James Joyce over Lawrence has not done much to enhance his visibility either. Yet in a map of modernism in which Ezra Pound and Wyndham Lewis are key landmarks and in which the profound links between literary and visual aesthetic innovation in this period are emphasised, Binyon assumes once more the importance he had in his own historical moment. Such a version of modernism has been tirelessly elaborated over the decades by Hugh Kenner, and we thus find Binyon resurfacing, in a modest way, in Kenner's magisterial study *The Pound Era*. 'Pound was the protégé ("bull-dog", he says rather) of Laurence Binyon (1869–1943) of the Department of Oriental Prints and Drawings.' And Kenner later elucidates for us a cryptic line – 'BinBin "is beauty"' – from Pound's *Cantos*: 'Binyon used to say "Slowness is beauty" at the Wiener Cafe, 1908; Pound has recalled not believing it then, but being unable to forget it until it yielded its beauty in slowness' (Kenner 1975: 236, 330).

Perhaps we should pursue these hints, to the point where Binyon's writings on Oriental aesthetics would come to seem as seminal as Ernest Fenollosa's *The Chinese Written Character as a Medium for Poetry* for modernist formal experimentation. Renewed attention to his art historical writings might even lead to a revival of his verse, from *Lyric Poems* (1894) onwards, which we should perhaps discover new ways of reading in the process; simply to get a cheap paperback selection out in print would be a great help, for a start. If Lancaster City Council has bothered to put up a commemorative stone to Binyon and to name streets after him, then it would seem appropriate that his 'local' university should undertake this project of revaluation and reprinting. And since research 'centres' are currently so much the name of the game, academically speaking, what we are really talking about here is, precisely, the Binyon Centre. This would involve a team of dedicated interdisciplinary scholars (literary *and* art-historical) collecting manuscripts and archive material, undertaking the definitive biography, bringing out a collected works with the full benefit of modern editorial techniques, putting together the cheap student paperback selection, organising a series of major international conferences which would reorganise the very history of modernism itself around their hero's work – supported all the while, of course, by great quantities of money from the central university administration, commercial sponsorship (local businesses proud of their local lad), the Chinese and Japanese embassies, and Lancaster City Council too. In my more fanciful moments, usually while basking in a hot bath after a particularly heavy jogging session, I occasionally construct this grand edifice, which of course includes a new Binyon Building to house its multifarious projects, down to the last detail and brick.

This formidable scheme will not, however, come to pass. Not just because the biographical links between Binyon and Lancaster are too flimsy (though they are – he moved to London as a boy), nor just because Binyon's work couldn't stand the weight of it (though this is probably the case), but because Lancaster University already has a grand scheme in progress: a 'Ruskin Programme' which will doubtless in the fullness of time become a Ruskin Centre. The notion of locality is important here too: Lancaster is the closest university to Brantwood, Ruskin's house and two-hundred acre estate in the Lake District where he lived from 1872 until his death in 1900. It will therefore, in due course, become the repository for an important collection of Ruskin manuscripts and drawings which have hitherto been housed at Bembridge in the Isle of Wight. Around this trove of material the university is constructing a project as ambitious as that which I sketched above in relation to Laurence Binyon. A programme of internal seminars and visiting speaker meetings is vigorously under way; a collection of its papers has been published (Wheeler and Whiteley 1992), and an exhibition on 'Ruskin, tradition and architecture' opened in the university art gallery in March 1992. Behind these immediately visible activities many longer-term projects are taking shape. The Ruskin Programme has become one part of the university's Development Campaign, which is seeking to raise £1½ million of sponsorship money in order to construct a new library building to house the collection and the range of editing and research activities which are planned around them. Situated on what is currently a bowling green, this new Ruskin Building will be, as it were, at the 'prow' of the university, the first edifice the visitor encounters as he or she drives up the hill to the campus. From its hilltop perch, it will have an impressive view across the local countryside, dominated as that is by the massive white cube of Heysham nuclear power station just a few miles away on the coast as the crow flies.

But there is, it seems, nothing particularly unique about Lancaster's project for a Ruskin Centre; this is, rather, the way we can expect university English departments in general to develop over the next few years. The closest parallel I know is provided by the D.H. Lawrence Centre which Nottingham University has established, and which was inaugurated by a conference on Lawrence's work in November 1991. In Lawrence's case, with the Cambridge edition, much of the editorial work which such a centre might undertake has already been done; but a rich array of other historical and literary-theoretical research projects is possible, and with a thriving D.H. Lawrence Society in Eastwood the Centre will have a local as well as academic base on which to build. It, too, like the Ruskin Programme, is now casting around for substantial sponsorship in order to erect a new building to house its activities and manuscripts. Like the Lancaster project, the Lawrence Centre has produced an attractive, glossy brochure describing its aims, which suggest that here too sizeable sums of internal money are 'pump-priming' both the academic activities and the quest for external funding.

Within a few years, it seems, any university which can lay claim to a 'local' writer (and, armed with *The Oxford Literary Guide to the British Isles*, there will be few indeed which are unable to do this) will be busily constructing a centre around his or her works. Such centres are likely to become a more and more dominant form for the institutional organisation of English studies; and in the age of literary theory and the poststructuralist 'death of the subject' that much-deconstructed figure, the author (or at least his or her Centre), proves suprisingly resilient after all. It therefore seems worthwhile reflecting a little on literary centres as a general phenomenon as well as on the two – Ruskin, Lawrence – which I have chosen to focus on here. Such centres are, one can speculate, a distinctively postmodern phenomenon, whether they know it or not. In their celebration of a local author and thus implicitly a regional culture – Ruskin's Lake District, Lawrence's Midlands – they clearly belong to the 'decentralist' moment of postmodernism, affirming the particular over and against the placeless universalism of modernist architecture (Le Corbusier, Walter Gropius). Within a more limited British context, this affirmation of the regional serves as a challenge to the hegemony of Oxford and Cambridge in the national higher education system; it constitutes, in Matthew Arnold's terms, a rebellion of the 'provincial' against the metropolitan urbanity, the 'tone of the centre', which Oxbridge is presumed to represent. Such literary centres, then, seem attractively democratic; they are part of that multicultural impulse currently under way in our society in terms of gender, sexual and racial as well as geographical identities.

However, the Eastwood D.H. Lawrence Society is one thing, and the University of Nottingham D.H. Lawrence Centre is quite another. The former has been gallantly organised by local enthusiasts on a shoestring budget for many years; the latter, with substantial internal funds behind it, cannot but be part of that transformation of the university system which has been so rapid over these last few years. Certainly the writer is still 'local' and the Centre, physically speaking, is situated in a specific place; but by virtue of being a university project it belongs to the increasingly internationalised and marketised culture of the higher education system at the end of the Thatcher decade. Raising local morale against the cool, distant sneers of Oxbridge is a welcome decentralism, but an equally important motif in that raising of 'local' profile is the desire to attract students and scholars, and thus their money, on a global scale. Japan, Germany and America, as the world's most powerful economies, will be particularly important here; and it is surely symptomatic that the Nottingham Lawrence brochure, distributed to those who attended the inaugural conference, quotes prices for the building it hopes to construct in American dollars. It is far from my intention here to be critical of this trend. At a time when our own government is starving humanities departments of funds, they need to be as resourceful as they can in seeking money and support from elsewhere; and the 'globalising' of student and academic life, mismanaged and economically driven though it is in practice, is surely in principle intellectually desirable. But I do want to stress the conceptual contradiction between the supposed 'localism' of the Centre and the increasingly integrated academic 'world system' in which it is coming into being. This contradiction, too, like regionalism itself, is a recognisably postmodern phenomenon. For the postmodern or 'late' capitalist economy operates, as many theorists have pointed out, simultaneously both 'below' and 'beyond' the confines of the old nation-state. All of us, and not just the directors of academic centres, are at the same time more pluralistically local and integratedly global than we have ever been before.[1]

Such contradictions are replicated at the practical level of the effects such centres have on the departments from which they emerge; but this is a level of detail I do not want to descend to here. I want, rather, to consider the uses to which the two centres I have focused on – Ruskin and Lawrence – might be put, the ways in which these ambitious projects might be articulated into the projects of a radical criticism in the postmodern epoch. The 'uses' I shall speculate on are perhaps far removed from those of the current directors of these institutions, but since the teams which run these centres must perforce tread a wary tightrope path between their own internal purposes and the wider contemporary cultural currency of Ruskin and Lawrence, an attempt to redefine the latter can hope to some extent at least to impinge practically upon those institutions themselves. I want to sketch a broader cultural project in which Ruskin and Lawrence, great precursors though they are, would be but Hegelian 'moments'.

The essential reason why a Laurence Binyon Centre makes little sense while a John Ruskin Centre makes a lot is not simply the fact that the latter is already under way while the former is my personal pipe dream (that's the contingent reason). It is, rather, that Binyon belongs by and large to a classicist culture which in its aspiration to universalist truths has no regard for the specificity of any particular place, while the notion of the 'Gothic' which is at the core of Ruskin's life work valorises locality and despises the classicism which despises it. To have a Binyon Centre in a particular place, as if he rootedly belonged to it, is thus an oxymoron, while in Ruskin's case it is consonant with the main thrust of the work itself. In his great chapter on 'The nature of Gothic' in *The Stones of Venice*, Ruskin relates Gothic architecture to place in two ways. It is, first, the fitting architecture for its native landscape, 'the North', a symbiotic link which announces itself in every last detail of 'this look of mountain brotherhood between the cathedral and the Alp' (Ruskin 1985: 82). But it is place-specific too in its inner creative impulse, in its character as social labour. Whereas classicist architecture operates in a 'top-down' mode, first taking shape as a perfect Platonic form in the architect's mind and only secondarily seeking a specific earthbound manifestation, the Gothic building comes into being 'from the ground up'. It is not the mere embodiment of a pre-given plan but rather takes form through the creativity of its workers; it is what *they* collectively make it, thus bearing the intimate imprint of their cultural and regional particularity. A similar valuing of place is apparent throughout Lawrence's work. Think only of the opening pages of *The Rainbow*, with their celebration of rooted *Gemeinschaft* in a few square miles of the English Midlands – so stark a contrast to that world of deracinated *Gesellschaft* or 'industrialism' which has come into being by the closing pages of the book. And *The Rainbow*, a novel which revolves slowly round that memorable encounter with Lincoln

Cathedral in chapter 7, is, as I have argued elsewhere, a novel that is Ruskinian through and through.[2]

Ruskin in Lancaster, Lawrence in Nottingham: these are locations which make 'theoretical' as well as practical sense. But it is the prior allegiance to a 'Gothic' critique of classicist universalism which leads to those particular, value-charged regions which are Ruskin's Lake District and Lawrence's Midlands. And these academic centres will, I suggest, only make their fullest intellectual sense if they are seen as ways in, through the exploration of particular lives and oeuvres, to the question of what a living 'Gothic culture' might be for us today. Beset as such projects are always likely to be by the twin dangers of hagiography and antiquarianism, the exploration of a viable contemporary Gothic, should they undertake it, will provide a vital counterbalance in favour of bold theoretical speculation and cultural–political engagement. And, indeed, it seems as though the kind of framework in which such an investigation could be fruitfully carried out is coming into being even as I write. For in the wake of the 'first Gothic conference' at the University of East Anglia (UEA) in 1991 an 'International Gothic Association' is now being established. A UEA flier announces that 'the goals of the association will be to promote further understanding of the gothic in literature, film, or other arts, through the circulation of a newsletter and through the holding of occasional (perhaps biannual) conferences . . . The next conference we hope will be held in Germany in 1992.' It seems, then, as if a whole new academic Gothicism is coming into being around us, with well-funded regional bases and a lively international network.

With all this going on, it seems important to ask what precisely 'the Gothic' means or, better, what it can be made to mean for us today, in the postmodern. In the brief compass of this chapter, I can only offer some very preliminary thoughts: three possible strands of meaning, one crucial problem for a contemporary Gothic, and a tentative hint or two towards its solution. The 'return to the Gothic' which, as we have seen, characterises some areas of academic literary studies today, is surely just one aspect of a more general cultural and political 'return'. In the postmodern 1980s and 1990s the Left has witnessed the intellectual implosion of Althusserian Marxism in the face of its poststructuralist challengers, the outflanking of traditional class politics by new forms of activism (ecology, feminism, gay politics, anti-racism) and, most recently, the utter collapse of Communism in Eastern Europe and the Soviet Union. In an unsettling postmodernist environment, socialists have been looking back to the premodern 1880s and 1890s for succour and inspiration. Our own post-Bolshevik era is looking again, in a spirit of *reculer pour mieux sauter*, at that pre-Bolshevik one, in which many of the new politics of the last few years which have had to emerge outside 'official' socialism (Leninist or Labourite) were then part of a rich, vibrant and popular socialist culture. The socialism of those years, still deeply infused by what we have come to term (after Lukács) 'romantic anti-capitalism', may well, in its many-sided critique of capitalist modernity, have more to say to our own postmodern epoch than the 'scientific Marxism' which mortgaged itself so deeply to the very modernity it believed it was challenging.[3]

The single most important representative of that earlier socialism (at least in Britain) is William Morris, who at last yokes the regressive anti-capitalism of Thomas Carlyle and John Ruskin to the contemporary labour movement. And the single most important and suggestive cultural legacy of that socialism is, surely, the concept of the Gothic – a notion which it powerfully reactivates in its own historical moment but does not, for all that, exhaust. The Gothic, then, is first of all the Gothic cathedral, that resonant image of lost *Gemeinschaft* and of a pleasurable labour process which funds the romantic critique of capitalism in the first place. From Morris on, it opens up the whole field of utopia, of a utopian rather than Engelsian 'scientific' socialism; and the re-emergence of such futuristic visions and desires – ecological, feminist and socialist – will be a crucial part of any progressive postmodern politics. Moreover, the Gothic in this sense – the cathedral and its builders – at once opens into questions of architecture, of built space and the city, the politics of place and geography, all of which have themselves made so dramatic a comeback in the 'postmodern geographies' of Edward Soja, David Harvey and others. The 1890s and 1990s, a utopian romantic anti-capitalism and our own 'depthless' postmodern culture, startlingly converge in what Soja terms the 'spatial turn' of contemporary radical thought and practice.[4]

But the Gothic is also a matter of sombre, louring mansions

rather than utopian cathedrals, of spaces of enclosure and paranoia rather than liberation, spaces where – as for Jane Eyre in Thornfield Hall – eerie laughter echoes terrifyingly around the third floor and a powerful, sinister, older male presides dolefully. The Gothic now, in this second sense, is 'female Gothic', in Ellen Moers's famous phrase: a proto- or actually feminist form of fiction all the way from Ann Radcliffe to Angela Carter. This may seem a far cry indeed from Ruskin's 'Of Queen's Gardens' and the demurely domestic women in the Hammersmith Guest House in Morris's *News from Nowhere*. For these two turbulent nineteenth-century counter-cultural impulses – the one raising crucial 'public' questions about community, labour, urban space, relations with the natural environment, the other addressing no less vital 'private' issues of gender relations, sexual power, desire, the psychoanalytical – remained the Adornian split halves of an integral Gothic culture to which, however, they did not add up, just as they continue not to today. But it would be a key task for a postmodern Gothic criticism to forge those absent links, in both theory and cultural practice.

These sinister enclosures then point us towards a third sense of Gothic: horror in general. For one of the most striking features of recent mass culture has been its pervasive 'Goth-icisation', the transformation of Gothic as a distinct sub-genre with its own highly formalised rules into the very texture of our mass-cultural existence. Or, as Noel Carroll puts it in his *Philosophy of Horror*,

> horror has become a staple across contemporary art forms, popular and otherwise, spawning vampires, trolls, gremlins, zombies, werewolves, demonically possessed children, space monsters of all sizes, and other unname-able concoctions that has made the last decade or so seem like one long Halloween night.
>
> (Carroll 1990: 1–2)

If it seems a long way from Lyonel Feininger's 'Cathedral of socialism' to Jonathan Demme's *Silence of the Lambs*, it would be precisely the task of a new Gothic criticism to measure and understand that distance, to articulate the political unconscious of the degraded or destructive Gothics of our own cultural moment and when possible to decode even there, within the very forms of contemporary horror itself, utopian impulses which may (however distorted) still faintly resonate.

Perhaps these three dimensions of the Gothic – utopia and space; women's writing; mass-cultural horror – constitute, in ways we cannot yet fully grasp, nothing less than a new academic discipline; perhaps, in the wake of an International Gothic Association, we shall soon be seeing BA programmes in 'Gothic studies' with David Lynch among the honorary degrees on graduation day. More modestly, the polysemous nature of the term 'Gothic', its implicit offer to link up diverse areas of our cultural and social being in ways which we have not yet worked through in theory and practice, may offer some opportunistic pedagogical advantages. In the epoch of academic 'modularisation', when what were once degree courses collapse into individually chosen shopping baskets of options, the very range of the Gothic may make it educationally as well as politically useful in its ability to articulate such diverse raw materials. Certainly this is its advantage at a postgraduate or research level, where it offers a way of constellating the potentially narrow biographical projects of a Lawrence or a Ruskin Centre in a field of study which becomes virtually coterminous with postmodern culture itself.

If a Gothic criticism is, in these assorted centres and associations, coming to birth in the postmodern, what exactly is its relation to the latter? Within the realm of architecture itself, there are deep parallels between the Ruskinian critique of classicism and the postmodern settling of accounts with International Style modernist architecture. But if the Gothic thus dovetails with some versions of the postmodern – around the themes of historicism, populism, decentralisation, ecology – there are other potent forms of postmodernity with which its articulation is much more problematic; all that is signalled, say, by such slogans as 'society of the spectacle', the 'logic of the simulacrum', image-culture, or the implosion of the social. For if the Gothic points to a pleasurable form of work modelled on artisanal craft-production as a critique of Fordist industrialism, how much mileage is left in this utopian vision in the age of fifth-generation computers, post-Fordist information technology and William Gibson's cyberpunk? This, above all, is the central problem confronted by would-be Gothicists today, who must demonstrate that Jean Baudrillard as well as

Jonathan Porritt has a place of honour on their bookshelves and that they are as cheerful jacking into a cybernetic matrix as they are dancing round a maypole in a Morrisian happy Hobbitland.

In the space left to me here I cannot confront the issue fully. But it should be possible, none the less, to evoke the continued suggestiveness of Gothic thinking within even an image-saturated consumerist postmodernism. Umberto Eco, in his two fine essays on 'The return of the Middle Ages' in *Travels in Hyper-Reality*, gives us a pointer in this direction when he asks, 'What would Ruskin, Morris, and the pre-Raphaelites have said if they had been told that the rediscovery of the Middle Ages would be the work of the twentieth-century mass media?' If this means merely that we admire Arnold Schwarzenegger's biceps and swordplay as we watch some regressive Dark Ages fantasy on video, it perhaps doesn't get us very far. However, a few pages later Eco more interestingly speculates not just that postmodernity avidly consumes images of medievalism but that the medieval itself was postmodern: 'The Middle Ages are the civilisation of vision, where the cathedral is the great book in stone, and is indeed the advertisement, the TV screen, the mystic comic strip that must narrate and explain everything' (Eco 1987: 81). In the closing phrases here the great romantic anti-capitalist motif of the Gothic cathedral undergoes an epochal metamorphosis, one which fully refits it for our own cultural moment. No longer an image of unalienated labour, as it was for Morris, or of utopian political aspiration, as for Feininger, it re-emerges, like Dr Jekyll after drinking his potion, as a vast electronic advertising image – one which makes the Tyrell Corporation pyramids and Off-World advertising drones in *Blade Runner* look like enfeebled distant echoes of its mightier self.

Eco throws this notion up in an essay that is packed with brilliant, casual *aperçus* ('the relationship between illuminated manuscript and cathedral is the same as that between MOMA and Hollywood'). But it is put to sustained work in Martin Pawley's rich study of *Theory and Design in the Second Machine Age*. Rejecting the best known formulations of a postmodern architecture, Pawley in this book is none the less impressively grappling with the question of postmodernism, above all with 'the information revolution, something that in the last decade has brought about a massive shift from an industrial to an information economy' (Pawley 1990: 123). This rapid shift to a post-Fordist economy has, he argues, led to a crisis in urban space, which becomes 'a disorganised multiplicity of sign systems tracking back through time, of which perhaps the oldest and most overlaid is architecture' (ibid.: 122). Upon an old industrial architectural infrastructure layer upon layer of new semiological systems appropriate to an age of mass media, advertising and information technology have been deposited. A fatal rift between architecture and the new social purposes and technologies it is serving opens up; an information avalanche threatens to descend upon us. The canonical postmodern 'solution' – hide the VDUs away behind a revivalist facade – is, Pawley argues, no solution at all but merely a restatement of the split in sharper form. The popularity of this version of postmodernism in his view proves 'our thinking in thrall to the idea that the product of our built environment should still be architecture and not information' (ibid.: 120).

Faced with this crisis of urban space, Pawley turns, as had William Morris before him, to the Gothic cathedral, but a Gothic made excitingly new and topical. The chapter of Pawley's book from which I am citing is called 'Information, the "Gothic solution" ', and in a remarkable postmodern rethinking of the structure and function of the cathedral he concludes, à la Umberto Eco, that:

> Coupled with the still astounding acoustic performance of these buildings, what remains of the imagery of their immense windows makes it clear that they were in fact total pre-electronic information systems . . . seen in this way Gothic architecture, otherwise a phenomenon shrouded in medieval mystery, becomes an information architecture.
>
> (ibid.: 115)

If this is flamboyantly to postmodernise the Gothic, Pawley is no less concerned to 'gothicise' the postmodern. The cathedral, that is to say, even in its new Baudrillardian guise, still carries a utopian charge which might altogether transform our fallen architectural present. Just as, for Ruskin and Morris, the Gothic dissolved the cruel social dualisms of planner and craftworker, work and pleasure, art and labour, so too for Martin

Pawley does the utopian force of his postmodern Gothic lie in the motif of reintegration. If the 'final disconnection of external form from internal function is the one architectural event of historic significance that can truly be said to have taken place in the 1980s', then we must instead dream of a new 'building type in which information and architecture are already nearly as perfectly integrated as in a Gothic cathedral' (ibid. 129):

> If the cathedral master builders found an architecture that completely expressed the information content of their culture, *mutatis mutandis* so can we. If the Gothic analogy is correct, the next step in architecture should be reintegration of the built environment with the overlaid information systems that have been allowed to take over its proper task.
>
> (ibid.: 123)

No doubt Martin Pawley's construction of the Gothic is open to debate from many angles: at one end of the spectrum there will be questions about historical evidence and 'philological' accuracy, at the other end arguments about those buildings he points to as partial instances of an 'informational-Gothic' solution (in my view they are in danger of reducing the notion back to modernism *tout court*). Yet in the end it is surely the vigour and audacity of this postmodern Gothic which impresses the reader of *Theory and Design in the Second Machine Age*, the recovery of the old utopian impulse in an extraordinary new form. No finer proof could be wanted of the continuing vigour of a Gothic cultural criticism, even in a one-dimensional society of the cyborg and the simulacrum. The task of a postmodern Gothic literary critic is to follow in Pawley's footsteps and, on the basis of the diverse energies of the Gothic tradition and supported by the various academic centres and associations, to invent a new form of Gothic culture which will be as richly diagnostic and predictive as Pawley's own.

NOTES

1 See further on this my (1991) *Raymond Williams: Postmodern Novelist*, Bridgend: Seren Books.
2 See my (1990) *D.H. Lawrence*, Hemel Hempstead: Harvester, ch. 2, 'Northernness and modernism', especially pp. 60–78.

3 For an excellent brief survey of the romantic anti-capitalist tradition, see Michael Löwy (1981) 'Marxism and revolutionary romanticism', *Telos*, 49 (Fall): 83–95.
4 See further on all this my (1990) 'Space: the final frontier', *News from Nowhere* 8 (Autumn): 10–27.

BIBLIOGRAPHY

Carroll, N. (1990) *The Philosophy of Horror: Or Paradoxes of the Heart*, London: Routledge.
Curtis, P. (ed.) (1991) *Dynamism: The Art of Modern Life Before the Great War*, Liverpool: Liverpool Tate Gallery.
Eco, U. (1987) *Travels in Hyper-Reality*, London: Pan Books.
Kenner, H. (1975) *The Pound Era: The Age of Ezra Pound, T.S. Eliot, James Joyce and Wyndham Lewis*, London: Faber & Faber.
Pawley, M. (1990) *Theory and Design in the Second Machine Age*, Oxford: Basil Blackwell.
Ruskin, J. (1985) *Unto this Last and Other Writings*, ed. Clive Wilmer, Harmondsworth: Penguin Books.
Wheeler, M. and Whiteley, N. (eds) (1992) *The Lamp of Memory: Ruskin, Tradition and Architecture*, Manchester: Manchester University Press.

6

PARADIGM LOST AND PARADIGM REGAINED

Antony Easthope

A fairer Paradise is founded now.
(Milton, *Paradise Regained*, book 4, l. 613)

Thomas Kuhn in *The Structure of Scientific Revolutions* (1962) argues that the production of knowledge within the natural sciences takes place within paradigms and that these paradigms change. Thus a science is held in place by a form of consensus; gradually evidence conflicting with its principles begins to accumulate and contradictions within its logic come to be noticed until not merely local details but the whole paradigm falls into question. There follows a period of what Kuhn calls 'abnormal science', during which the larger theoretical questions kept on a backburner while the consensus was maintained come into direct discussion. After this a new paradigm emerges from the criticisms of the old, a fresh consensus is established and things return to normal.

It is instructive to envisage what has happened to literary studies over the past generation as following by analogy the process Kuhn describes. The former paradigm was established especially during the years after 1930 in Britain and North America. And it was not until the 1960s that various aspects of it came under serious attack. There ensued, on classic Kuhnian lines, a return to 'first principles' and – on the model of book VI *Paradise Lost* – the great 'theory wars' of the 1970s and early 1980s which laid waste the known universe of literary study. Not necessarily of value in itself, the moment of theory was a symptom of a wider crisis. However, partly in the spirit of a polemical optimism which affirms as already real what it wishes to see come about and partly to test the implications for theory of the Kuhnian possibility, I shall outline briefly a shape for the new paradigm. I shall also try to contrast it with the old by putting alongside each other two pieces of criticism, both dealing with E.M. Forster's *A Passage to India*.

PARADIGM LOST

What follows is an abstracted and hypostasised version of the old literary studies paradigm. Of course this was nothing like a completely unified or homogeneous set of beliefs about literature and how to teach it – but then you do not have to have complete agreement to have a consensus and a sustainable paradigm. Even if F.R. Leavis holds up the consensus in his way at one side and Kathleen Raine in a very different way at another, they both can be claimed to participate in 'the general will' of paradigm-support until an explicitly different and opposed paradigm comes along. So, arguably, across variant positions literary studies was structured by five features:

1 Epistemological empiricism – that is, the assumption that the text was a given, a free-standing object, available more or less directly to unprejudiced observation and experience. An instance of this would be Leavis's oft-cited willingness to describe his procedure as sustaining one side of a dialogue in which someone says, 'This is so, isn't it?', and your friendly interlocutor replies, 'Yes, but . . . ' (It is a sign of the underlying arms of the consensus that Leavis never considered what would happen if you said, 'No, absolutely not!') Another would be the way, in a varied inflection, W.K. Wimsatt and Monroe Beardsley treat that which their famous title names as 'the verbal icon'. A choice recent example was provided by James Wood in the *Times Literary Supplement* (7 June 1991), affirming that literature 'is its own best theory' and so the best criticism 'would let, as it were, literature interpret itself' (the momentary hesitation of that 'as it were' at the prospect of a copy of *Hamlet* walking past interpreting itself is one for real connoisseurs of critical cant). This epistemology was foundational for literary studies because it placed the reader – and the reading – outside and in subordination to the text. The reader's job (R)

91

was to respond imaginatively to or experience the text (T) as already given. Thus: T ← R.

2 The method of the modernist reading. This was the assumption, developed especially by William Empson and I.A. Richards between 1927 and 1930, that the text was intransitive and therefore that all aspects of it were to be examined as possible contributors to some overall theme. Borrowing the term from Jane Tompkins, I call this the modernist reading and will not say more about it now because I mean to illustrate it with the examples of Forster criticism below.

3 The high cultural canon. Literary study came into existence via a gesture which divides the high cultural literary canon from popular culture (popular novels, film, radio, later television and video). This therefore provides a field for literary study to demarcate as its own (and to revere, often explicitly, always implicitly, by denigrating its supposed exterior, popular culture).

4 The literary object. The immediate object of literary study was the canonical text revealed as such by the modernist reading (all plausible paradigms contain such internal elements of self-confirmation).

5 Textual unity. This was often 'imaginative' unity, derived from Kantian aesthetics and Romantic organicist criticism, though it took on board a much older assumption that art depended upon unity (however defined). It is crucial to the paradigm that the text is seen as unified (or to be unified), because this view of the text as (always already) complete confirms that it is a self-sufficient object which is accordingly available to an empiricist epistemology. The contrary possibility makes the effect clearer: if the text is not inherently unified, then it requires the reader to complete it in their reading (but admit that and the conventional paradigm begins to sink under you).

On occasions when the old paradigm is challenged people often say things like, 'Why can't we forget about all this theory and just read literature?' The number of such protesters has come to include (Sir) Frank Kermode, who in a recent article (*Guardian*, 10 October 1991), in the very act of acknowledging that books cannot talk about themselves nevertheless appeals to the notion of 'literary works in themselves' in the course of attacking subscribers to the new paradigm for 'an indifference to literature, an ignorance of what it is to read it, even a denial that it genuinely exists'. These 'literary works in themselves' are of course texts as constructed by the old literary studies paradigm, that is, as canonical objects, imaginatively unified, supposedly existing as empirical givens. Literature 'itself' only exists when the paradigm for thinking of texts in this way has been so completely assimilated that it is forgotten.

THE PARADIGM IN CRISIS

Of the many causes for the demise of the literary studies paradigm far and away the most powerful has been the widespread acknowledgement in the West in the twentieth century that empiricism simply did not work as it was supposed to. One would surmise that this intellectual process has been inseparable from a larger political and cultural feeling that Western identity can no longer assume itself to be a self-evident norm, since it is really only one relative to many others, that in any case what has passed for the West's sense of itself has been covertly a masculine sense of itself in contrast to a denigrated feminine identity. Such larger questions apart, the development of philosophy in the West since 1900 traces its history in the recognition that knowledge depends upon the 'language games' in which it takes place (and Kuhn's intervention of 1962 may best be seen as part of this process). However, it was the Marxism of the 1960s which gave political edge to the critique of empiricism. For example, in 1972 in a famous essay on 'History: the poverty of empiricism' Gareth Steadman Jones argued that:

> Those who tried to create theory out of facts, never understood that it was only theory that could constitute them as facts in the first place. Similarly those who focused history upon the event, failed to realise that events are only meaningful in terms of a structure which will establish them as such.
>
> (Steadman Jones 1972: 113)

Jones derives his argument in part from E.H. Carr's *What is History?* (1961), in part from Althusser's critique of empiricism and corresponding argument that knowledge is constructed in the process of a theoretical practice.

Carried across to study of the text this rejection of empiricism entailed admission that the text does not exist in itself outside criticism of it, and that such criticism could not take place at all except on the basis of a theory of literature, whether this was explicitly avowed or remained hidden (as it had come to be in the literary studies paradigm). Further, if texts simply do not interpret themselves then they remain incomplete, in need of the reader and the reading to give them a semblance of unity (arguably, human beings as speaking subjects cannot manage without conferring some sense of imaginary unity on the world they experience). It was left to Pierre Macherey to proclaim this new understanding of the text's actual insufficiency, which he did in 1966 by italicising the following words: '*The postulated unity of the work which, more or less explicitly, has always haunted the enterprise of criticism, must now be denounced*' (Macherey 1978: 78). If one wished to put in diagram form the essential difference in the structuring of the new paradigm, this would be done by changing T ← R to T ↔ R, the double-headed arrow thus acknowledging that the text reads the reader as much as the reader reads the text.

Though it took a little time to tease it out, the consequence of Macherey's (not unprecedented) move was to devastate first the notion of the unity of the text (two down and three to go) and then, by implication, the text as canonical object (confirmed as such when its imaginative unity was revealed by the modernist reading). As for that modernist reading, the idea of reading for significance in every aspect of the text persists in the new paradigm but with a difference: if such reading can never end in a moment when the text reveals its completeness, where can it – and the reading – ever terminate? Closure then has to be sought in another direction, that is in an explicit acknowledgement that it follows from the context of interpretation the reader draws on for constructing the reading. The modernist method is carried forward into the new paradigm, but only because it becomes something else.

Epistemology, method, object, textual unity – with the rejection and revision of each of these the field of literary studies becomes eroded at its limit. This was (to recapitulate) the opposition between the canon and its other, between the high cultural work and the popular cultural text. No empiricist epistemology, no self-sufficient text; no autonomous text, no textual unity; no unity, no canonical object; no canon, so no credible opposition between the study of literature and the study of popular culture. In this domino effect it is the field of studies which has most visibly changed, the new paradigm thus (perhaps) earning a new name: not literary but 'cultural' studies.

There are other ways of telling it, but the story of the critique, crisis, collapse and transformation of the old paradigm can as well be recounted around the breaching of opposition on which the study of literature (and definitely not popular culture) was founded. In the middle of the 1960s it was the effect of a structuralism derived from linguistics to draw attention to the text as sign system (so continuing to signify for the reader even after the death of the author). There were attempts, notably that of Althusser in his 'Letter on art' (1977), to revive Russian Formalist accounts of how some linguistic feature inhered in the text – certain texts – and made it indelibly a part of literature; these were all unsuccessful, and so the construction of the text through linguistic theory helped to nullify the high culture/popular culture divide. So did theories of ideology introduced – more accurately, reintroduced – into literary studies after 1968. No sense was apparent in which the literary text could be set apart from its popular rivals on the grounds of a different and privileged relation to ideology. As for ideology, so in the early 1970s for theories of gender. Feminism has proved itself particularly adept at riding irreverently across the line between high and popular culture to show that gender meanings inhabit Hardy's *The Dynasts* as fully as they do television's *Dynasty*, that Sherlock Holmes stories and perfume advertisements can be read on the same terms as *The Winter's Tale* and *The Mill on the Floss* (see Belsey 1980).

The next wave in critique of the old paradigm was in some ways the most intimately damaging to it, for after 1973 (to give a date) and Roland Barthes' *The Pleasure of the Text*, psycho-analysis entered – re-entered – the arena of textual studies. It did so in ways I shall attend to in more detail in considering my illustrations, but what in particular it adds to the paradigmatic assumption (T ↔ R) is the reader's unconscious positioning in his or her reading and the possibility that the text performs for the reader as a fantasy scenario and the narrative of a wish-fulfilment. Canonical and non-canonical texts can both do this on equal terms, and so, for example, Lacanian psychoanalysis can be drawn on happily to discuss Hollywood cinema and the novels of Joyce (see MacCabe 1978 and 1985).

The work of Raymond Williams, Richard Hoggart and Stuart Hall – British cultural studies, as it has come to be called – provides another term for the new paradigm through its critique of the text's siting, its production and reproduction through social institutions. Although high cultural objects and the text of popular culture circulate through different institutions, typically state institutions for the canon and capitalist institutions for its popular other, the concept of institution to frame questions about audiences and the reception of a text applies with equal force to both.

Sign system, ideology, gender, identification and subject position, institution: the conceptual terms which performed the demolition of the old paradigm by the same critical gesture went to construct the new. Not simply eclectic or pragmatic, the new terms emerged from a coherent movement of critique, one held together by a concern for the politics of the text. And, structured around the double-headed arrow specifying an inescapably dialectical relation between text and reader, they constitute an avowedly poststructuralist paradigm, one, that is, in which no term is originary, none foundational. That they are thus imbricated in a decentred structure rather than erected hierarchically upon a foundation might be instanced by the ease with which they could accommodate themselves to the insertion of other conceptual terms (the other, for example, or questions of ecology). Terms for the new paradigm might be summarised as follows:

1 A theoretical epistemology. The text exists in its interpretations, themselves known to be inseparable from theoretical assumptions.

2 The method of the modernist reading. This lies in some continuity with the literary studies paradigm, with the difference that it cannot claim to reveal the significance of the text except as this is provisionally given by the admitted purposes of the reading.

3 The field of cultural studies. What were formerly construed

as canonical texts are read alongside the works of popular culture in a single field of study.

4 Protocols of reading. Sign system, ideology, gender, subject position, institution (as above), each (and potentially others) sanctioned by the necessity that without a context of reading there is no reading.

While no one would pretend that the new paradigm is evenly in place or institutionally established, a consensus has emerged, as a contrast between two readings of *A Passage to India* by Lionel Trilling (1944) and Sara Suleri (1987) may hope to show, expanding, testing and qualifying these sketchy preliminary remarks with specific instances.

A PASSAGE TO INDIA: TRILLING AND SULERI

Trilling

In his 'Introduction: Forster and the liberal imagination', Trilling relates his reading of Forster to a liberal tradition which he defines (implicitly against Marxist views – the date is 1944) by saying we must reach beyond a sense of merely social and 'class-conditioned action' to an assumption of a person's 'essential humanity' (Trilling 1944: 18). This is the acknowledged context for the reading of *A Passage to India*.

There is not a great deal to say about the details of Trilling's account, because its procedures are so widespread and familiar, both inside and outside the academy (in higher journalism, some television programmes), that they seem to be merely common sense. Trilling begins with several pages on the historical author's experiences of visiting India, Forster's journalism of the period and his anxieties about censorship. *A Passage to India* is said to be a very 'public' novel in which Forster 'has put himself to the test of verisimilitude', posing questions such as:

> Is this the truth about India? Is this the way the English act? – always? sometimes? Never? Are Indians like this? – all of them? some of them? Why so many Moslems and so few Hindus? Why so much Hindu religion and so little Moslem? And then, finally, the disintegrating question, What is to be done?
>
> (ibid.: 125)

This material is, nevertheless, all 'under the control . . . of the author's insight' (ibid.: 123) and his 'social imagination' (ibid.: 124), so that a 'pattern' is established and kept to, a pattern regulating how we give and withhold our sympathies from the characters in the novel (here Trilling summarises the plot and describes some of the characters). The novel proceeds on 'an imperialistic premise', that the English have thrown away the possibility of holding India because of 'the undeveloped heart' (ibid.: 129), and so a 'sense of separateness', dividing races, sexes and cultures, 'broods over the book, pervasive, symbolic' (ibid.: 130). Incidents, dialogue, characterisation develop this theme in a 'web of reverberation' which gives the book 'a cohesion and intricacy usually only found in music' (ibid.: 134). Dominant among these 'echoes' is the echo in the Marabar caves, which Trilling reads in terms of the inadequacy of Christianity and the question of Hinduism, connecting these to 'separateness':

> Certainly it is not to be supposed that Forster finds in Hinduism an answer to the problem of India; and its dangers have been amply demonstrated in the case of Mrs. Moore herself. But here at least is the vision in which the arbitrary human barriers sink before the extinction of all things.
>
> (ibid.: 137)

This is a nub and it is important to be clear about what it says. For Trilling, Hinduism as represented in the echoes of the Marabar caves means 'the extinction of all things'; this vision is necessary and good because in its face 'arbitrary human barriers', differences of race, sex and culture, become nullified so that a sense of universal human nature can emerge. Hence his conclusion to the chapter: Forster's book 'is not about India alone; it is about all of human life' (ibid.: 138).

Striking here, to a contemporary reader, is Trilling's unruffled assumption that the text is as intricately cohesive as music, when this unity apparently holds together so many different discourses and forms of discourse: journalism, political commentary, novelistic narrative, the representation of character, dialogue, pervasive symbolic material, the thematic assertion of a universal human nature underlying separateness.

This presumed unity is a necessary condition for the empiricism of Trilling's method, though, as will be argued, *A Passage to India* is seen as 'given', simply there, only through a curious paradox by which as a text it hardly has any material existence at all.

Knowledge is possible because a means of representation makes an object available to a subject. Entirely typical of conventional literary criticism (see Belsey 1982), Trilling's empiricist method works through a number of superimpositions, in each of which any means to represent an object for a subject becomes effaced.

Thus the first is the real, in this case 'the truth about India', which is apparently carried directly across into textuality: *A Passage to India* contains 'an enormous amount of observation of both English and native society' (Trilling 1944: 128), is an 'investigation' (ibid.: 130), full of 'data' gathered for it (ibid.: 129). No means of representation is visible for this given (datum), which is assumed to be simply objective, factual and existing outside interpretation – in Trilling's term, 'public'. In the text it sits alongside other material which is admitted to have a means of representation in that it is subjective and a form of personal interpretation, namely, the sense of separateness which 'broods over the book, pervasive, symbolic', the 'web of reverberation' around the echo, the 'vision' of human nature. Nevertheless (the second superimposition), the 'truth about India' passes directly through this interpretation, in fact passes into it to become amalgamated with it. Even the most 'public' material is worked into a unity by 'Forster's social imagination' (a fine phrase, uniting a subjective faculty with the objective world of society). Objectively, then, there is the world of the novel (the 'truth about India' now modified by Forster's interpretation); subjectively there is us, the readers of the novel, who are faced with the problem of getting from the means of representation to what the novel represents for us. Not, however, in this critical conception. For in a further translation (the third superimposition), the text of the novel passes directly into the experience of its readers, with only minor interference. This is shown in Trilling's use of the familiar trope of conventional criticism in which the author speaks (in the present tense) and 'we' are said to respond, also in the present tense (ibid.: 136, 137).

In Trilling's account there is simply no material distance or difference between object and subject and no problem introduced by the means of representation. Object and subject are made for each other – mirror each other – in the reproduction of the real as text, of 'facts' as interpretation, of the whole novel in and for a reader. One sign of this is a seemingly marginal but actually crucial use of metaphor, the 'web of reverberation' and the textual 'echoes' of the Marabar caves incident (and the same happens, I think, in the way a persistent metaphorisation of Indian landscape from the novel is drawn on to say that separateness 'broods over the book'). In each phrasing a representative feature *within* the text is drawn on *outside* the text as a means to interpret it, so eliding the disjunction between text and interpretation, giving the effect that the text, as it were, interprets itself.

How is this done? Because 'E.M. Forster' is available as a mediating term between object and subject; 'Forster's social imagination' can negotiate between observations of India on one side and on the other a vision in which 'arbitary human barriers sink before the extinction of all things'. It can do so the more easily because it derives from human nature (no explanation is given of how this 'E.M. Forster' came about), its object (the truth about India) exemplifies human nature and the novel is about 'all of human life'. Something gets missed in this closed reciprocity in which objective human nature and inward human nature reflect each other. *A Passage to India*, all 317 pages, does not exist at all as writing, as a bundle of discourses with their own formal, linguistic properties. The novel is given, there, because it is merely transparent. 'The acts of imagination by which Forster conveys the sense of the Indian gods are truly wonderful' (ibid.: 125): thus the novel exists only as a pane of glass does for light passing through it or as an oil tanker does for oil – it 'conveys' something else.

Suleri

A good point of departure for talking about Suleri's subtle, clear and accomplished reading may be that at which it marks itself off from Trilling. He recolonises the mental geography of the text by offering it as 'a humanely liberal parable for imperialism', interpreting the novel's depiction of Eastern action 'as a metaphor for the behaviour of the West', so that 'the only difference of India inheres in the fact that it is symbolic of something the western mind must learn about itself' (Suleri 1987: 170). Quite. When Trilling concludes that the novel is about 'all of human life' he means, of course, the European Enlightenment tradition.

Suleri does refer to 'Forster' but it is evident from her usages ('Forster manipulates the image of landscape' – ibid.: 173) that this 'Forster' names the avowed project not of a personality but of a text, the official reading *A Passage to India* can be seen to offer of itself (and which Trilling thinks is all there is). So for Suleri the novel is not a unity but rather is divided against itself, just as the manifest content of a dream differs from and disguises the latent content.

> While *A Passage to India* ostensibly centres on a hysteric who believes she has been raped, the course of the narrative suggests that the real outrage lies in the fact that this rude encounter has been withheld from her. India diffuses into emptiness before it completes the seduction it had promised, as though its own formlessness demands that it can be master of only an incomplete performance.
>
> (ibid.: 171–2)

How, in a Machereyan inflection, the text can be made to speak what it denies is developed and explored across three domains.

One is that of sexuality and desire. The novel's surface endorsement of the horror of the rape conceals another level at which the rape is wished for and its non-completion regretted, a level at which the female figures in the text are disparaged and the male ones desire and are desired. So Suleri can argue that 'Adela essentially plays the part of a conduit or passageway for the aborted eroticism between the European Fielding and the Indian Aziz' (ibid.: 174), with blame for that impenetrability being projected back on to Aziz.

This is projected on to Aziz but also projected on to India. For Suleri reads the text explicitly in relation to Edward Said's *Orientalism* (1978). In arguing that the West has constructed the East as an object to know and master, and so as the other it needs to define itself, Said suggests how the Oriental other functions for the Occidental imagination as an object of desire and what Suleri terms 'a figure of seduction' (Suleri 1987: 171). Resisting this mastery just as Aziz refuses Fielding's covert invitation, India comes to be construed by the novel as empty and vacuous, so that 'Mosque', 'Caves' and 'Temple' function precisely as 'cavities to contain western perceptions of that which is missing from the East' (ibid.: 172). But in Suleri's third domain, *A Passage to India* is divided against itself as textuality and representation. These 'cavities' the novel finds in its attempted representation of India disclose the 'fictionality' (ibid.: 169) which inevitably generates fear in the (Western) determination to find truth in the real, to resolve ambiguity into absolute certainty, to reduce difference to the same. The fact of writing – which entails that a final meeting is always deferred – undoes Forster's project (according to Trilling) of telling 'the truth about India': but this failure is recuperated by being cast back on to the object the text tries to master as India's failure.

For Suleri, then, *A Passage to India* is a book not about India but 'about the representation of India' (ibid.: 169), a text concerned with how meaning may be textualised. And it is fully consistent with this that her own text does not claim a status it denies to Forster's. So it explicitly situates itself in relation to certain theoretical perspectives as its conditions of possibility – to Orientalism as analysed by Said (and formally named) but also, through its deliberate terminology and frame of reference, to psychoanalysis and to Derridean deconstruction. Suleri hardly needs to say – though she does – that she wishes 'to present a reading' (ibid.). Consequent on this conscious framing of the analysis is the recognition that *A Passage to India*, far from being a unique text, is just one instance of more widespread codes and structures, specifically 'the mode' (ibid.: 169, 170) by which a British text represents India, West represents East. Although Suleri does not directly confront the high culture/popular culture opposition, her writing refers Forster's novel to codes and ideologies potentially at work across the range of representations of the East. Her reading could as easily be applied to that television advertisement for chocolates 'full of Eastern promise' and associated with night, sheikhs and tents, so setting *A Passage to India* in the enlarged field of cultural studies.

Again, it goes without saying that Forster's novel is not read here in terms of the canon of EngLit. It cannot be, because Suleri treats it not as a given but as the effect of a process of construction so that it remains incomplete – except as it is completed by her chosen (and provisional) theoretical context (without this, the reading could never end). That the text is an address to a reader is specifically acknowledged by the terminology of fantasy employed – the novel partakes of a mode which conceals an 'obsessive fear' (ibid.: 169); it is 'secretly obsessed with the desire to describe' (ibid.: 170). In these ways Suleri's Forster partakes of the new paradigm, T ↔ R.

Suleri is attentive to *A Passage to India* at the level of sign system and text. She does not draw on the concept of ideology but clearly accedes to the view that shared forms of social power are exercised by Forster's novel. She persuasively relates questions of gender to both a reader's possible positioning and identification in the text. And though she does not overtly designate the novel in terms of social institutions of readership she writes very strongly about the textual institution the novel initiates (referring it, for example to Naipaul's *An Area of Darkness*). The epistemology is theoretically explicit; there is a modernist reading in which all details are assumed to signify, though these are not then funnelled into a supposed centre in the unity of the text. What my account has so far not mentioned is the brevity and confidence of the analysis, which I take to be not just personal but symptomatic. Compared to the moralising impressionism of the old lit. crit., this is a reading which believes it has a better politics as well as being able to give a better close reading of the text. It is able to do both because there is now a better paradigm which makes such a reading possible.

BIBLIOGRAPHY

Althusser, Louis (1977) 'A letter on art' in his *Lenin and Philosophy*, London: New Left Books, 203–8.
Barthes, Roland (1976) *The Pleasure of the Text*, London: Jonathan Cape.
Belsey, Catherine (1980) *Critical Practice*, London: Methuen.
—— (1982) 'Re-reading the great tradition' in Peter Widdowson (ed.) *Re-Reading English*, London: Methuen, pp. 121–35.
Carr, E.H. (1961) *What is History?* London: Macmillan.
Empson, William (1930) *Seven Types of Ambiguity*, London: Chatto & Windus.

Kuhn, Thomas (1962) *The Structure of Scientific Revolutions* (2nd rev. edn 1970), Chicago: University of Chicago Press.

MacCabe, Colin (1978) *James Joyce and the Revolution of the Word*, London: Macmillan.

—— (1985) *Theoretical Essays*, Manchester: Manchester University Press.

Macherey, Pierre (1978) *Theory of Literary Production*, London: Routledge & Kegan Paul.

Richards, I.A. (1929) *Practical Criticism*, London: Chatto & Windus.

Said, Edward (1978) *Orientalism*, Harmondsworth: Penguin.

Steadman Jones, Gareth (1972) 'History: the poverty of empiricism' in Robin Blackburn (ed.) *Ideology in Social Science*, London: Fontana, pp. 96–115.

Suleri, Sara (1987) 'The geography of *A Passage to India*' in Harold Bloom (ed.) *E.M. Forster: Modern Critical Views*, New York: Chelsea House, pp. 169–75.

Trilling, Lionel (1944) *E.M. Forster: A Study*, London: Hogarth.

Wimsatt, W.K. and Beardsley, Monroe (1970) *The Verbal Icon: Studies in the Meaning of Poetry*, London: Methuen.

7

THE TERGIVERSATIONS OF EMINENT FEMINISTS

Maggie Humm

Virginia Woolf quoted Bertrand Russell in *Three Guineas*:

> 'Anyone,' writes Bertrand Russell, 'who desires amusement may be advised to look up the tergiversations of eminent craniologists in their attempts to prove from brain measurements that women are stupider than men.'
>
> (Woolf 1939: 159)

> 'If they have lied about Me, they have lied about everything.'
>
> (Walker 1989: preface)

INTRODUCTION

In April 1989 the University of Liverpool hosted a Cixous Colloquium. The name of the event encapsulates its aim: to introduce a conversation between French feminist writing and teaching and British feminism. Cixous' double, two hour-long lecture 'therapies' were models of feminist theory, ranging as they did through psychoanalysis, history and culture.

A few months after this event in 1989, and dare I say passed over in the feminist academic journals, Alice Walker came to the Africa Centre in London to read from her novel *The Temple of my Familiar*. It was a heady evening. The hall overflowed with power-dressed Black women; many more, unable to squeeze inside, chanted 'Alice, Alice' through the cracks in the door. Before the evening's reading, a newly born baby girl was named Abena in a ceremony from the Ashanti region of Ghana. The ceremony was a moving celebration, with songs of praise and a pouring of libations to Alice Walker and to her familiar, to honour queens everywhere and especially to girl children born on a Tuesday and therefore, like Alice Walker herself, also called Abena.

Like the Cixous Colloquium, the evening can be seen to stand synecdochically for a whole way of understanding how creative writing and theory and teaching give our lives meaning. Yet it was the addition of another event in 1989 which brought these issues about feminist theory and women's studies more directly to me. The year 1989 was the seventieth anniversary of the publication of two key texts of British philosophy – Bertrand Russell's *Introduction to Mathematical Philosophy*, containing his theory of types, and Russell's 'On propositions: what they are and how they mean', which focuses on the meanings of experience.

Now it may seem unnecessarily complicated to include in a chapter on feminist theory and women's studies the incompatible synthesis of a Cixous Colloquium and an Alice Walker reading, to speak of women's studies and Bertrand Russell. But I want to suggest that the Cixous Colloquium on the one hand and the Alice Walker reading on the other can be viewed through the unlikely prism of Russell as images of two alternative forms of contemporary feminist theory. And because I am having to write and teach feminist theory shaped by my experiences in one camp but desperate to resist the privileging of academic theory over feminist creativity located largely outside the academy in the other camp, I want to claim that women's studies must incorporate both in a more 'monumental' space (to use Kristeva's term from 'Women's time') (Kristeva 1992). The two kinds of feminist theory, then, that I am describing are, first, the various feminist speculations about types of historical women, women's bodies (in debates about sexuality), which are deeply concerned with questions about women's language (écriture feminine). These speculations have their 'politics of location' in the silent pages of *Feminist Studies* or *Differences* and in the quiet rooms of higher education where journals are discussed. Second, there is what I could call a creative model which uses myths, narratives and metaphors expressing an interpretative grid of theory and experience, a model we can see in Alice Walker's novel. That 'gulf' between white theory and Black creativity/theory has involved Alice Walker and Audre Lorde and others in a radical questioning of the relationship between language and experience, an investigation into new means of knowing. Any question about means is a question of theory.

By assuming that experience is represented in the forms of languages which philosophers use to write about their worlds, and can be deconstructed, feminists often ignore their own daily realities and those of other women. Current white feminist theory is in debt to discourse analysis, the method which French critic Michel Foucault and others use to demonstrate how power works in society through its different languages. What discourse analysis describes are the categories society uses to 'capture' experience, not the ways in which experiences might be actually felt or shared. Women's activities, religious feelings and sensations are therefore not always best captured by philosophical categories. The question, which I believe Black feminist writers answer very well, is how to create a theory within which women might identify our lives and experience.

Some of the most important theoretical writing emerges in creative texts. Alice Walker's writing seems to me a particularly pertinent model of the way fiction can foreground different political/theoretical arguments by juxtaposing different forms of language. For example, *The Temple of My Familiar*, as I shall describe later, is a complex story which mixes the spiritual narratives of people speaking in tongues with historical accounts, autobiography and dreams in order to confront the theoretical problem of representing women's bodies, heterosexual practices and racial and sexual violence from different political perspectives. Another, and equally vivid, example is the work of Gloria Anzaldúa, who deliberately organises whole books, for instance *Making Face, Making Soul: Haciendo Caras*, into what she calls a method of poetic association where readers 'join the dots' between poems, autobiography and political statements to awaken our feelings about racism and homophobia (see Anzaldúa 1990: xviii).

Of course, white academic feminist theory has itself not avoided the fictitious voyage. For example, there is the superb transition between autobiography, history and feminism in Du Plessis' 'For the Etruscans' and Carolyn Steedman's *Landscape for a Good Woman*. Thus although white academic feminist theory has begun more accurately to conceive of women in the plural, less in a universal concept of female identity and more as a density of different sexualities, races and classes embedded in particular social and historical fields, the need for some holy water, some feminist phenomenology bottled at source, is a feverish thirst. There is something odd and profoundly troubling about theoretical positions that emphatically reject essentialism yet recreate symbolic universals whose imperatives appear inescapable. For instance, many white deconstructionists writing about sexuality (such as those published in *Pleasure and Danger*, edited by Carol Vance, as I shall argue in a moment) claim that radical feminists like Sara Ruddick, who celebrate maternal nurturing and 'preservative love', are too essentialist.

Creating a typology of ultimates and types limits feminist inqury. What is being left out is the realm of poetry, religion and ethnicity. The exaltation of types demands a simplistic notion of identity based on the fiction of a coherent self. Briefly put, then, the theoretical advances in white academic feminist theory, and they are major, constantly threaten to swallow in the process of knowledge-creation the imagination of Black, Asian and women of colour and, even worse, exclude their presence. In 'but some of us are (still) brave . . .', a report on Black women in the American academy, Yolanda Moses points out that while Black women constitute 59.6 per cent of the total Black enrolment in 1990, Black women's share of doctorates was down to 5.4 per cent from 8.7 per cent in 1976 and Black women constituted 1.9 per cent only of full time faculty (see Moses 1990). Similarly in Britain, a recent Commission for Racial Equality (CRE) report discovered that in most institutions of higher education the employment of black staff is at a minimal level. In an analysis of replies to a questionnaire soliciting evidence of equal opportunities policies, the report concludes that the majority of universities and then-polytechnics have barely begun thinking about the issues. It concludes: 'a tone of moral superiority or complacency plus ignorance of the issues was pervasive' (Williams *et al.* 1989: 24).

The limitations of America's and of Britain's more elitist education have a vivid economic parallel in the figures of 25,000 Bangladeshi homeworkers in London's East End or the EC estimate that 70 per cent of European cleaning jobs are held by Black women (Islington Women's Equality Unit 1991).

The economic and educational conundrum of difference was skated over by the less reflexive analogy of race/sex made by pioneering second wave feminists such as Kate Millett, Simone de Beauvoir and Shulamith Firestone. To name 'woman' was a precondition for that feminist moment of solidarity. The experience of Blacks, to these writers, had a similar caste-like status, so that the triple jeopardy of racism, sexism and classism could not be conceptualised. As Deborah King points out in 'Multiple jeopardy, multiple consciousness', even the introduction of such concepts is simplistic, since a simple incremental model cannot represent the nature of Black women's oppression. It is not just that economically, racially disadvantaged women have not been recognised in most white feminist theories about identity and experience, and thus the multiple and creative ways in which Black women address the issues of triple jeopardy in their daily lives have not been considered, but white feminist theory devalues Black women at the conceptual level – for example, in Nancy Chodorow's exclusion of race and class in 'the reproduction of mothering' (Chodorow 1992).

Now certainly the fact of these two alternative forms of feminist theory is not peculiar to this year, nor is my highlighting of them particularly original. Hazel Carby, for instance, argues that most feminist theory 'does not begin to adequately account for the experience of black women' (Carby 1989: xviii). But she goes on to claim that since it is not simply a question of absence, then we cannot 'in any formulaic way articulate the two discourses of race and gender' (ibid.). Unlike Carby, I believe that 'articulations', or what I would call 'confrontations', however 'formulaic', are crucial in women's studies to enable us to understand the histories and practices of the very different constituencies of women – Bangladeshi, Hindi, Black and white lesbian – often asserting their presence in our classrooms. Consequently I want to begin with an admittedly schematic account of current feminist theory using Russell as a paradigm and then set up the specific synchronicity of the Cixous Colloquium and Alice Walker's work.

THEORIES OF TYPES

So how does white academic feminist theory address this politics of knowledge? My signpost Bertrand Russell might be a warning. I am not proposing that Russell's philosophy is at all compatible with feminist theory, but I do want to flag Russell as a warning. The philosophical study of language, according to Russell in his *Introduction to Mathematical Philosophy* and 'On propositions', was expected to provide nothing less than the metaphysician's goal of understanding the structure of the world. With the publication of Russell's work, British philosophy took a linguistic turn, involving itself with the analysis of moral rules, universalism and forms of thinking. Russell's general philosophical aims were threefold: to devise a theory of types; to search for the ultimate constituents of the world; and to conceive the outline of an ideal language. To the day of his death, Russell persisted with the idea that the properties of language would help us understand the structure of the world. These beliefs would now be generally agreed by feminists to represent a white, middle-class, masculine perspective. Yet Russell's dream is not far removed from feminist theory's utopian aims of types of unalienated women, the ultimate constituents of their bodies and an ideal language in which they can speak. White feminist theory's attempt to wash women clean from misogynist stereotyping is not unlike Russell's aim to be free from all philosophical defects which mar ordinary language. Russell claimed that his language would be 'completely analytical and . . . show at a glance the logical structure of the facts asserted or denied' (Russell 1919b: 520).

Yet it should no longer be big news that deconstruction, poststructuralism and postmodernism should have demystified our ideas of universal types. The assumption that there is some essentially truthful relation between language, reality and integrated selves is challenged by postmodernism's mixture of past and present. Postmodernists claim that 'fictions' are useful concepts, not just constructs, of knowledge. Postmodernism, in the work of Jean-Françoise Lyotard and Jean Baudrillard, is based on the proposition that language is eclectic, a mixture of popular and historical forms with no universal authority. In postmodern fiction, for example Gayl Jones's *Corregidora*, the narrator contests her historical boundaries. Ursa Corregidora has to define her experience of sexuality in a battle between her memories of Corregidora, the nineteenth-century slaveowner who fathered both her mother and grandmother (Jones 1988). However, if we look closely at the major responses to postmodernism from current feminist theory, those of Alice Jardine in *Gynesis* and Donna Haraway in 'A manifesto for cyborgs', despite the fact that both seem to want to escape from universalism, we can see how one of Russell's aims – a theory of types – is eternally in play in these texts.

What Jardine is analysing in *Gynesis* is the breakdown in master narratives amid the discursive routines of modernity, postmodernism and contemporary French and Anglo-American feminist theory. *Gynesis* is Jardine's term for a process she discovers in French thought where slippages or 'spaces' are represented as feminine. The reason this breakdown has occurred, Jardine argues, relates to what she calls 'denaturalization' or the proof by Derrida, Lacan *et al.* that ideology is based on naturalised categories. Jardine strategically defines the crisis as one of figurability. For example, Jardine shows how European writing 'confronted with systems of production and belief foreign to its own' (Jardine 1985: 92) retreats into its own boundaries. The space outside is always described as the Other or woman because this space often carries 'feminine connotations' (ibid.: 88). One of the strengths of Jardine's work is her compelling mapping of the feminine as the 'space' or absence in male texts. But this discursive strategy poses its own problems, since Jardine finally suggests that feminist forms of address be attached to 'identities' of types of women, even if these are necessary fictions.

Donna Haraway is also in debt to postmodernism yet also wishes to assert a theory of types: 'my taxonomy which like any other taxonomy is a reinscription of history' (Haraway 1989: 184). Her essay was first published in *The Socialist Review* in 1985 in response to a call for political thinking about the 1980s from a socialist-feminist perspective. Although, like Jardine, Haraway contests a feminist dream of a common language as 'totalising', she too focuses on a type of woman – the cyborg. Haraway defines her cyborg as a cybernetic hybrid of machine and organism. 'It is oppositional, utopian, and completely without innocence' (ibid.: 175). By the 1990s, Haraway claims, we are all cyborgs – theorised and fabricated hybrids. Only feminist cyborgs can break with the complex system of technologies encircling the globe where 'the nimble fingers of Oriental women' (ibid.: 178) depend intimately, like commercial pornography and religious evangelism, on computing electronics. In a strategic move, Haraway avoids confronting essentialism by disappearing at the close of the essay into feminist science fiction and its ideal types. For example, she cites Orca in McIntyre's *Superluminal*, a genetically altered diver who can speak with killer whales but longs to explore space as a pilot, while McCaffrey's *The Ship Who Sang* has a cyborg hybrid of girl's brain and complex machinery. In mourning for her lost past of Marxist humanism, Haraway has created a Jacksonian Rainbow coalition of metaphorical counter-identifications and, like Jessie Jackson, vividly sets her world of types in a rhetoric of evangelism where she speaks about salamanders and global knowledge. Even Bertrand Russell would shudder at Haraway's technological determinism and I shudder at her 'nimble fingers of Oriental women', however facetiously intended.

Where Haraway looks outwards and upwards for her angelic cyborgs, Denise Riley in *Am I That Name?* looks backwards into a veritable archaeology of historical women. The book is an attempt to conceptualise types of women in a way that avoids essentialism. Riley argues that while the biological 'woman' has a continuous history, the history of 'women' is discontinuous – discursively and historically constituted. Yet history, Riley claims, and she is a historian, will need to be a full history of feminisations. 'It will be a lengthy and cumbersome task', perhaps like Russell's lifetime devotion, if we are, as Riley has it, to 'track all the slow and powerful consolidations which name sexes and which must be pursued' (Riley 1988: 139).

Teresa de Lauretis's work, like that of Jardine, Haraway and Riley, represents a remarkable effort to impose theoretical coherence on the miscellaneous identities of fluctuating women. Suiting practice to theory, de Lauretis adds the visible to Riley's historical and Haraway's technological figurations. In *Alice Doesn't* and *Technologies of Gender*, de Lauretis addresses conflicting representations of historical, fictional and visual women. Lauretis's main thesis is that subjectivity, or ideal types, are constructed through practices of representation in cinema and in politics. Joining Jardine, Haraway and Riley in a consensual assertion that identities are constituted by a historical process of consciousness, de Lauretis formulates an ideal type, neither gynesis nor cyborg but one who 'individually can interpret her own history in self-analysing practices' (de Lauretis 1987: 186).

The advantage of all these theories of ultimate types is that they construct women from various historical practices and languages while at the same time recognising the fallibility of these discourses. From the other side, the problem with constructed individuals is that they seem to deny collectivity and dialogue in favour of an inviolable intentiality. These feminist theories of types are shot through with the idea that history is linear – often finding subjects lagging behind contemporary history or far ahead of it. Always, and out of sight, are other types – which are radical, more fundamentally feminist. This can lead to an excessive optimism about knowledge, as if truth can be manifest and therefore a failure to find truth is an intellectual sin. Similarly, Bertrand Russell (1973) proved to himself that it was possible to have the perceptive experience of 'seeing a cat' even if no physical cat was present. If I replace cat with 'woman' in Russell's tale, his little story bears an uncanny resemblance to Riley's temporalities of women.

Suppose I see what I take to be a woman and answer the question 'What is that?' by saying, 'That is a woman.' If I am asked, 'are you quite sure?', I may well, knowing that there are such things as dummies, page three women, flat posters of a convincingly *trompe d'oeil* character and so forth, answer, 'Well, it looks like a woman,' or, 'It appears to be a woman.' What I mean here is that it has the more or less directly visible properties of a woman. But more than this has to be true of a feminist woman proper. A feminist must have been *Of Woman Born*, move herself about in *No Man's Land*, use genderlects or *Silences*, eat anorexically or bulimically or so on to be a feminist woman rather than a phenomenological description of my immediate experience (Rich 1977, Gilbert and Gubar 1988, Olsen 1979).

Alice Walker's operative verb, on the other hand, might be 'lie'. As she says in the epigraph to *The Temple of My Familiar*: 'If they have lied about Me, they have lied about everything.' (Walker 1989: preface.)

THE CONSTITUENTS OF BODIES

For feminism, the universal constituents of women's bodies – to use another of Russell's terms – like the universal types of women, is an issue that will not go away. For feminism, the most common source of knowledge has historically been the

113

constituents of bodily experience. Under conditions of oppression and victimisation, the feminist psychoanalyst Jean Baker Miller argues, women, like all oppressed groups, develop skills and strengths such as dependency which are currently devalued but which correctly credited and promoted as 'creative interaction' can form the constituents of a feminist world (Baker Miller 1992). Carol Gilligan similarly, in *In a Different Voice*, discovered that all the women she interviewed irrespective of class, race, or age had an agreed conception of the world which was different from that of men. Whereas men saw the world composed of autonomous separate beings, women saw people in interdependence. Men therefore create a moral universe built from rights and duties while women, Gilligan perceives, focus on responsibilities and needs (Gilligan 1982). Gilligan's faith that women have special capacities which it is feminism's responsibility to catalogue, finds an echo in white feminist discussions about sex.

The great weight of a feminist theory of the ultimate constituents of women bears down most heavily on sexuality. Debates about the ultimate constituents of women's sexuality, its pleasures and dangers, have long been the focus of contemporary feminism. The Barnard Conference of 1982 is a good example of taxonomic theories being deployed in order to establish sexual convictions. At Barnard an argument erupted between feminist anti-pornographers and feminist lesbian sadomasochists. In *Pleasure and Danger*, Carol Vance collected papers from that debate. In these, while some feminists described quantifiable groups, others wished to expel the chimera of 'normality' through a hugh inventory of sexual practices (Vance 1984).

In part, this struggle about representations and sexual practices is about the ultimate and appropriate constituents of a feminist sexual world. Are women intrinsically responsible and gentle sexual beings, meaning that sexual violence must be the term for rape and harassment? Or does woman's sexual desire signal a host of intra-psychic and physical activities setting in play representations of power, strength, even violence that were formerly taboo or 'masculine'? On the other hand, if sexuality is socially constructed, then sexuality *can* be reconstructed or deconstructed into ultimate feminist constituents. This geopolitics of feminist sexuality, and debates over lesbian sadomasochism or butch fem roles as appropriate constituents of that politics, assumes a theory of direct description which denies the indirectness of the causal link between the constituents of sexuality and women's perception of it. The assumption is that sexuality must be in one place or in another. As Audre Lorde has pointed out, many Black women are not in a position to 'debate' about their bodies when they continually work their bodies to satisfy the needs of whites (Lorde 1984).

AN IDEAL LANGUAGE

One could illustrate at length the positivities and fallacies in both these appeals to types and to constituents of experience but I wish to highlight briefly the third mode of current white feminist theory – the search for an ideal language. In America Mary Daly and in France Luce Irigaray and Hélène Cixous have been influential proponents of this search. From their very different perspectives they focus on the ideal qualities of femaleness. For Daly in *Gyn/Ecology* and most spectacularly in her 'Dictionary' (Daly 1978, Daly and Caputi 1987), there are gender-specific traits of language which flow from a gendered ontology. A-mazing Crones will be able to break the 'mind binding power' of words because it is in language, patriarchal language Daly believes, that deceptive perceptions are implanted (Daly 1978: 368). This feminist journey is a creative crystallised 'gynocentric manifestation of the Intransitive verb' (Daly 1978: 23).

The French feminist Luce Irigaray has, in an unabashed way, recognised aloud that any attention to women must admit the degree to which sexual identity is conditioned by language. Irigaray's erotics of writing in recent work like *Amante Marine* (Irigaray 1980) finds a language in elemental metaphors of earth, air, fire and water which provide a truer materiality of women's discourse. As she said as early as 1977, 'there should no longer be separation: sex/language on the one hand, body/matter on the other. Then perhaps another history would be possible' (Irigaray 1977: 76). In *Speculum* and *This Sex Which is Not One*, Irigaray set out to quote from, to absorb, to appropriate into the feminine, particular philosophers – Nietzsche, Heidegger, Levinas – so that Irigaray's language is not only metaphorically feminine in itself but transmutes these masculine

imaginings and fears into a different poetics. If Irigaray somewhat resembles the heteroglossial Fevvers of Angela Carter's
Nights at the Circus, she does display the 'female' as a disruptive,
deconstructing, fabulous figure.

Hélène Cixous constitutes this figure in the marginalised
languages of the mad, the irrational, the maternal and the
hysteric. Cixous emphasises her belief in the necessity for an
ideal language based on the distinctiveness of women's bodies.
Cixous holds to the conviction that there is a potential common
essence to a 'feminine' text. Her now familiar devices for
revealing the feminine are her use of particular signifiers, for
example beginning a sentence with 'with' to create a fluid,
feminine syntax, or the use of a word from another language to
prevent the bourgeois ownership of a text. The key question
for these seekers after a discursive Holy Grail is what shape we
can give to a 'female' language which avoids the collapse into
the stereotypical female with its reproduction of patriarchal
images of femininity. Russell's claim that 'every proposition
which we can understand must be composed wholly of constituents with which we are acquainted' is an absurd and
salutary warning to those who argue that the language which
women can understand must be wholly composed of constituents, say body images, with which we are acquainted
(Russell 1919b: 91).

So why read and write feminist theory anyway? Why bother
to establish the existence of women by argument? A woman is
a woman is a woman. The answer to these questions is that we
need theory not only to describe women's experience but to
show that certain recognisable features of our experience have
properties (of maternity or discrimination) which require these
features to be emphasised again and again as philosophically
important. These questions concern the very foundation of all
knowledge and feminist theory enables us to acquire, nouveau
riche, an embarrassingly realistic volume of systematic information about ourselves. But in the last few years white
feminist theory, it seems to me, has begun to embody the
regressive features of much traditional philosophy: its
emphasis on abstraction and devotion to logical perfection. We
should be cautious of creating a kind of thinking which
influenced the production of such articles as G.E. Moore's
famous 'Is existence a predicate?' (in Moore 1959).

BLACK FEMINIST THEORY

In Alice Walker's *The Temple of My Familiar*, in Shabnam Grewal *et al.*'s *Charting the Journey*, Barbara Smith's *Yours in Struggle*, Audre Lorde's *A Burst of Light* and Gayatri Spivak's *In Other Worlds*, spoken moments are sites of resistance. In asking 'Can the subaltern speak?' Spivak answers no, not in any unproblematic sense. If the perennial question is one of ultimates and their epistemology then Hortense Spillers' essay, 'Notes on an alternative model: neither/nor', offers a model of displacement. Looking at the semantic markers of the mulatto in Faulkner's *Absalom, Absalom* and other novels, Spillers compares literary with actual historical subjects who were sold in 1736 for 'gunpowder and sheets'. Spillers is radically opposed to the ultimate constituents of languages and types which determine racist beliefs and practices. The mulatto is difference at its most extreme as the specular object of the gaze of white imperialism. Spillers creates a theory of difference through very dispersed configurations. She is concerned with strategies of substitution and containment. What Spillers does so brilliantly here, and in her other writing, it seems to me, is to attack the lack of movement in the field of feminist signification. Spillers is not refusing one discourse – the canonic literary mode – in favour of another – Black women slaves and their history – but enacting what Foucault called an 'enunciative field' where different representations are set in discursive relation (Foucault 1977). This is hugely relevant, of course, for project work in women's studies, where we can involve students in similar collective fields, as I shall describe in a moment.

In 'The political economy of women as seen by a literary critic', Gayatri Spivak pertinently starts with another question: how does a literary critic read a paper at a feminist conference given that the condition of women is fractured by the international division of labour? Spivak's question can serve as a key to what I am taking to be the major point of difference in feminist theory – highlighted as the gap between April 1989 and Cixous' Colloquium, and September 1989 and Alice Walker's reading. Spivak's general strategy is to multiply articulations of discontinuity to underscore the particular interests served by languages. What Spivak dedicates herself to in *In Other Worlds* is the mighty and shattering task of changing the 'subject', not simply looking for ultimate types, ultimate constituents or an ideal language. Where Haraway uses the single term 'cyborg', Spivak multiplies differences – among women in the First World, between women in First and Third Worlds, between empiricists and theorists. Variety, multiplicity, different eroticisms are difficult to control. But to these writers the connections between different areas of knowledge in relation to Black female experience are paramount.

One of the first and path-breaking statements is Barbara Smith's *Toward a Black Feminist Criticism*. In this much anthologised piece Smith sets out to establish the contours of Black women's writing and its forms of representation. There are several givens in Smith's text which are very attractive and far different from the easy slide into 'gender' criticism now troubling at least this feminist critic. The most important is that theoretical discussion must be an ideologically inspired reading of difference, as Smith demonstrates so effectively in her reading of Toni Morrison's *Sula* as a Black lesbian novel. It is Black feminist writers who have seized on the idea that feminist theory is a political responsibility (Smith 1977).

Barbara Christian's essay 'The race for theory' illustrates this point. Christian's argument, as her title suggests, is that the critical world, by which she means the American academy, has been taken over by the 'race' of professional theory-creating critics, and this white academic hegemony has silenced women of colour, symbolised for Christian by the term 'minority discourse'. As she points out, Black women are central to much writing in the world, not marginal (if not in the American academy). Christian turns from her critique of white academic theory to 'theorizing' the creative writing of Black women poets and novelists. Black women have continually speculated theoretically about the world, she argues, although for the most part in stories, proverbs or what Christian calls 'hiero-gylphs' – forms different from Western logic. Consequently Black theory has not been recognised by the academy, just as Black people have been refused entry to its institutions. Christian is describing a critical representation of the startling and depressing statistics which I quoted earlier. Christian is not attacking theory in the simplistic way that Mary Evans so accurately castigated it in her essay 'In praise of theory'. Christian is not positing some intuitive truthful ultimate type, experience or language against theory but rather argues that theory has been 'co-opted'. She refuses to diminish theory by corrupting it into method. Theory should not become mere coins in an academic marketplace – of value only for its profitability in reading literary texts. 'I am tired of being asked to produce a black feminist literary theory as if I were a mechanical man' (Christian 1989: 227).

If we adopt the contrary course plotted by Smith, Spillers, Lorde and Christian, following analogies and metaphors, we rediscover a feminist theory that is more imaginative than descriptive, more emotional than rational. What one discovers is a fluid process, a movement of feminist meaning embodied in images. One good example of this vitality is Audre Lorde's *A Burst of Light*, where the image of light discloses to Lorde and to her reader certain celebratory identifications. Audre Lorde was a poet/theorist and self-proclaimed 'Black lesbian feminist socialist mother of two' (Lorde 1984: 114). She believes that concepts of difference in much of white feminist theory trivialise the power and creativity in 'the chaos of knowledge' (ibid.: 111). As the title of her essays *Sister Outsider* makes clear, Lorde believes we should juxtapose and celebrate differences, not deny them, if we are to begin to name ourselves. At the Sapphire Sapphos, a table laden with food is transmuted into a 'dreamlike fullness of women sharing color and food and warmth and light – Zami come true' (Lorde 1988: 51). Lorde immediately juxtaposes this image against the violence of medecine, using the word 'light' colloquially: 'In the light of all the reading I've been doing these past weeks . . . I've made up my mind not to have a liver biopsy' (ibid.: 54). The meaning of 'light' here is not incompatible with its earlier usage but jars us into tears at Lorde's courage and tears, too, at the absence of light which she needs to describe her body in order to save it. Without light 'cancer survivors are invisible to each other, and we begin to be invisible to ourselves' (ibid.: 127). Similarly, there is no 'light' at a women's writing conference she attends in Melbourne because Lorde cannot 'see' the daughters of Black Aboriginal women in her audience. Lorde's book is a very good example of what bell hooks calls the Black 'performative'. This is a form of writing/speaking which 'performs' with style and creativity the 'underclass experience that is devalued in academia' (Childers and hooks 1990: 78).

Work in Black women's studies, for example *Sister Outsider*, *This Bridge Called My Back*, *Borderlands*, and in Britain *Charting the Journey* (Lorde 1989, Moraga and Anzaldúa 1981, Anzaldúa 1987, Grewal *et al*. 1988), consolidates a creative epistemology built on distinctive experiences not available to other groups. The material positions occupied by ethnic women are not only, or even, those of domination or victimhood but stimulate a unique feminism usually defined as a both/or perspective. This is the act of being simultaneously a member of a white categorised social group and yet with very concrete experiences overflowing with self definitions (whether from the church or the family) which are uniquely different. For example, Alice Walker's knowledge claim in *In Search of our Mothers' Gardens* is that the Afro-American 'call and response', or testifying dialogue, is a very special interactive epistemology of connectedness with deep roots in African culture. Many of Walker's pivotal images of women are drawn from African oral literature and myth. For instance, 'womanist' has links with the Yorùbá deity Òṣun, a strong fertile woman. For Afro-Americans the emotional expressiveness of the oral tradition is a power not available to white women authors of books called *Silences*.

The Temple of My Familiar reveals Alice Walker's commitment to spirits and to prophecy and her move, expressed earlier, 'away from sociology, away from the writing of explanations and statistics and further into mystery, into poetry and into prophecy' (Walker 1984: 8). Her heroine Lissie has existed in past lives as a white man and as a lion and Walker's message is one of 'parent knowledge', of listening to ancestral voices rather than to formal education. So Fanny, for example, resigns from women's studies to become a masseuse, believing that physical, more than intellectual, contact is a source of healing. By the end of the novel male, as well as female, characters succeed in re-entering traditional modes of thought. Since Walker's message is that prehistorical African spirituality survives and is perpetuated in the culture of women, her work is a powerful feminist theology, which subjects Black culture to the authority of feminist issues. Similarly, in *The Color Purple*, part of Celie's liberation is her spiritual freedom from traditional Christianity. It is Celie's friendship with a bisexual, economically independent Black woman which leads to 'spiritual experience'. Walker makes explicit in the novel the notion that women best change our theories by bonding with other women. Shug tells Celie that God loves all their sexual feelings, and Celie's transformed notion of God recognises the divinity as neither male nor female but as a spirit inviting Celie to create a personal archaeology of liberation (Walker 1982). This spirituality, which Walker suggests is buried within us to be realised by attention to the natural world, is in sharp contrast to the shortcomings of white feminist theory. In Walker's work the responsibility for change is always given to women artists, weavers and musicians, not to academic thinkers, and in *In Search of our Mothers' Gardens*, Walker enlarges definitions of art to include quilt-making, baking and gardening.

By reading Walker's and Lorde's writings in the context of myth and religion we can begin to understand other ways of knowing. This emphasises the connection between what Gayatri Spivak calls the verbal and the social text. Appeals to spiritual experience need not be essentialist or ahistorical, because Walker tells us that the experience of Afro-American women is polyvalent. This is a 'different' kind of theory, one that is familial and testimonial. As Audre Lorde has so profoundly argued, 'it is often in poetry that we imagine that which we have been afraid to imagine – that poetry is an important source of imagining new ideas for change' (Christian 1989: 73). When Lorde calls herself *Sister Outsider* she is claiming a tension between identities and creating a connection between two apparently contradictory positions. This is often the condition of women's studies.

Black feminist writers and critics like Walker and Lorde are playing with possibilities. In their work we find a feminist theory that is more imaginative than descriptive. It is not surprising, although it is instructive, to find questions of ultimates and types addressed in more creative ways by Black feminism than by white feminist theory. These questions cannot be resolved, however, by appeals to difference alone as a cure for white feminism's myopia and racism. Nor can it help women's studies in Britain to devise realistic and creative curriculae when separatism is not, even if it should be, an option. It is all too easy to escape into a simple pluralism which, while it replaces institutional misogyny with an equal opportunities policy, none the less ignores the effects of the designation 'Black'.

If I have correctly mapped these alternative models of recent feminist theory, what do these tangents imply for women's studies in our courses as well as in our institutional places? What then of feminism as a teaching practice? The main challenge is to answer Spivak's question – a question that is very hard for a white feminist to answer 'performatively' in practice. Perhaps it cannot be directly answered but needs to be rephrased with reference to concrete instances, both actual and putative. I am also trying to face, I think, Spivak's or Christian's argument that a retrieval of the political economy of Black women in women's studies involves more than just adapting the curriculum.

If women's studies exist to help erode the home comforts of academic institutions, then the local zone of women's studies can only work with confrontations, with contestations, that might help us negotiate (as Spivak, Lorde, Smith and others so brilliantly do) the distances between Black, Asian and white women. All these critics confront in different ways the issue of 'otherness' and how theory might explicate it. In some sense this is the issue of women's studies. If women's studies is to be the 'enunciative field' of 'otherness', then it needs certainly to be continually enacting and critiquing languages. Just to give one obvious example: students can become involved in detective work tracking down a term, a signifier like 'Pakistani' in their local area where irreducible difference is flagged in the lodging cards in newsagents' windows. They can plot the borderline between Asian and 'Paki' in relation to contemporary British politics and a media which 'equips' all Asian women with signifiers of arranged marriages. They can compare all this with dreams we each detail and share while making the maps, and with the vivid metaphors described in novels like *A Wicked Old Woman* (Randhawa 1987) and in proverbs we collect from our mothers and grandmothers. In *A Place To Stay*, London theatre group Age Exchange collected powerful autobiographies by senior citizens in one local area who were originally from Pakistan. Women remembered songs they sang as children, while food such as chappatis stood for 'race' almost like the symbol of resistance in Palestine of picking wild thyme.

In women's studies, when we bear down hard on such a

micro-history, what Foucault might call the 'by-ways and margins' of history, it shocks us all. In citing the Alice Walker evening at the outset and to some extent posing it against or in confrontation with white academic feminist theory, I wish to suggest that the contest is political as well as theoretical, racial as well as social, and the issue for women's studies is whether we want to centre on race. I believe that this is crucial to perceiving where we are now as feminists and teachers of women's studies and where we might want to go.

To return to my beginning, in one women's studies class we read Alice Walker's 'A child of one's own'. The piece is auto-biographical and about Walker's entry into a Black identity as a Black woman professor and mother. By working openly on an emotional level, the piece prevents us from viewing racism as removed from ourselves or as a process in which we apparently do not personally participate. The piece is about integrity and creative freedom in culture, language and in academic curriculae. All Alice Walker's writing is theoretical and pedagogical as well as being full of dialect, punning and Black humour. When students chart similar cognitive processes of self-identification, not simply the theoretical ultimates of experience, types and language, around similar ruptures of oppression and political struggle, then our classrooms are more open to the power of theory as a craft and as an instrument. For example, all of us, white and Black, can make a historical critique of our positions, of what it means to be constructed in one language and suffer the violence of movement into another language, the language of education which often has no place for the subjectivities of the first. Yet while this might be said to be the speaking condition of all women to some extent, the notion of Black diaspora is a distinctive experience.

I think I had already realised that organising women's studies around teachable chunks, such as thematic representations of 'women and the family', 'women and sexuality', trying to give a balanced account – one week Asian, one week Afro-Caribbean – had its limitations. The study of Africa as a rhetorical figure in Walker or Lorde, for example, its sign of intuitive knowledge, its 'live' notion of continuous cultural moments, needs a more integrated vision. We can also 'read' the 'text' of the classroom as a collection of moments of social, historical and pedagogical ruptures, confrontations and differences. For instance, even with the most obvious 'shared' topic of violence against women, the violent racism experienced by our Black women students walking down Deptford High Street on a football match evening towers over neat academic statistics of domestic violence. The shift in contemporary white feminist theory from an emphasis on consciousness-raising and lifestyles to linguistic models is problematic. The Deptford example shows how we need always to integrate personal emotions and experience with feminist ethics and politics. Yet this also can carry a danger for the woman telling her story. The act of witnessing, of telling it like it is to a mixed audience, implies a distancing, seeing myself as oneself, for example as a homogenous Afro-Caribbean speaking for all Afro-Caribbeans – what in the nineteenth century, as Gayatri Spivak says, would have been called a 'Native Informant'. The question of representation, of self-representation, is a problem, not a solution. For me, the issue is not how and why we speak but how and why we listen; and how the speaking, autobiographical experience must be listened to as an issue of politics, of mobilisation as much as of consciousness, of theoretical problems, not ethnographic simplicities. Far better to start with what words, what theories are essential to Black women's self-discovery and hence survival. The study of Black women's writing – of Walker, Lorde, Spivak – becomes, then, part of a larger understanding of the role of language in human behaviour rather than one of ideal types or scripts, requiring a radical reassessment of how race and language, theory and writing, operate in society and for each of us. To the extent that women's studies is the systematic confrontation of differences, then women's studies might avoid being merely 'the tergiversations of eminent feminists'.

BIBLIOGRAPHY

Age Exchange (1984) *A Place To Stay*, London: Age Exchange Co.

Anzaldúa, Gloria (1987) *Borderlands*, San Francisco: Spinsters Press.

—— (ed.) (1990) *Making Face, Making Soul: Haciendo Caras*, San Francisco: Aunt Lute Books.

Baker Miller, J. (1992) 'Toward a new psychology of women', in M. Humm (ed.) *Feminisms: A Reader*, Hemel Hempstead: Harvester.

Bulkin, E., Bruce Pratt, M. and Smith, B. (1984) *Yours in Struggle*, New York: Long Haul Press.

Carby, Hazel (1989) quoted in E. Weed (ed.) *Coming to Terms*, London: Routledge.

Childers, Mary and hooks, bell (1990) 'A conversation about race and class', in M. Hirsch and E. Fox Keller (eds) *Conflicts in Feminism*, London: Routledge.

Chodorow, Nancy (1992) 'The reproduction of mothering', in M. Humm (ed.) *Feminisms: A Reader*, Hemel Hempstead: Harvester.

Christian, Barbara (1989) 'The race for theory', in L. Kaufman (ed.) *Gender and Theory*, Oxford: Basil Blackwell.

Cixous, Hélène (1988) 'Extreme fidelity', in S. Sellers (ed.) *Writing Differences*, Milton Keynes: Open University Press.

Daly, Mary (1978) *Gyn/Ecology*, London: Women's Press.

Daly, M. and Caputi, J. (1987) *Webster's First New Intergalactic Wickedry of the English Language*, Boston: Beacon.

Du Plessis, R.B. (1992) 'For the Etruscans', in M. Humm (ed.) *Feminisms: A Reader*, Hemel Hempstead: Harvester.

Evans, Mary (1983) 'In praise of theory', in G. Bowles and R. Duelli Klein (eds) *Theories of Women's Studies*, London: Routledge & Kegan Paul.

Foucault, M. (1977) *Language, Countermemory, Practice*, ed. with introduction by D.F. Bouchard, trans. D.F. Bouchard and S. Simon, Oxford: Basil Blackwell.

Gilbert, S.M. and Gubar, S. (1988) *No Man's Land*, New Haven, Conn.: Yale University Press.

Gilligan, Carol (1982) *In a Different Voice*, Cambridge, Mass.: Harvard University Press.

Grewal, S., Kay, J., Landor, L., Lewis, G. and Parmar, P. (1988) *Charting the Journey*, London: Sheba.

Haraway, Donna (1989) 'A manifesto for Cyborgs', in E. Weed (ed.) *Coming To Terms*, London: Routledge.

Humm, Maggie (ed.) (1992) *Feminisms: A Reader*, Hemel Hempstead: Harvester.

Irigaray, Luce (1977) 'Exile', *Ideology and Consciousness*, 1: 62–77.

—— (1980) *Amante Marine de Friedrich Nietzsche*, Paris: Minuit.

—— (1985) *Speculum of the Other Woman*, Ithaca, NY: Cornell University Press.

—— (1985) *This Sex Which is Not One*, Ithaca, NY: Cornell University Press.

Islington Women's Equality Unit (1991) *The Effects of 1992 and the Single European Market on Black, Migrant and Refugee Women*, London: Islington Women's Equality Unit.

Jardine, Alice (1985) *Gynesis*, Ithaca, NY: Cornell University Press.

Jones, Gayl (1988) *Corregidora*, London: Camden Press.

King, Deborah (1989) 'Multiple jeopardy, multiple consciousness', in M.R. Malson, J.F. O'Barr, S. Westphal-Wihl and M. Wyer (eds) *Feminist Theory in Practice and Process*, Chicago: University of Chicago Press.

Kristeva, J. (1992) 'Women's time' in M. Humm (ed.) *Feminisms: A Reader*, Hemel Hempstead: Harvester.

de Lauretis, Teresa (1984) *Alice Doesn't*, London: Macmillan.
—— (1987) *Technologies of Gender*, London: Macmillan.
Lorde, Audre (1984) *Sister Outsider*, Trumansberg, NY: Crossing Press.
—— (1988) *A Burst Of Light*, London: Sheba.
Moore, G.E. (1959) *Principia Ethica*, Cambridge: Cambridge University Press.
Moraga, Cherríe and Anzaldúa, Gloria (eds) (1981) *This Bridge Called My Back*, New York: Kitchen Table Press.
Moses, Yolanda (1990) '. . . but some of us are (still) brave', *Women's Review of Books*, 8(5), February: 31–2.
Olsen, T. (1979) *Silences*, New York: Dell.
Randhawa, R. (1987) *A Wicked Old Woman*, London: Women's Press.
Rich, A. (1977) *Of Woman Born*, London: Virago.
Riley, Denise (1988) *Am I That Name?* London: Macmillan.
Russell, Bertrand (1919a) *Introduction to Mathematical Philosophy*, London: George Allen & Unwin.
—— (1919b) 'On propositions: what they are and how they mean', *Proceedings of the Aristotelian Society*, 7: 1–43.
—— (1973) *An Inquiry into Meaning and Truth*, Harmondsworth: Penguin.
Smith, Barbara (1977) *Toward a Black Feminist Criticism*, Trumansberg, NY: Out & Out Press.
Spillers, Hortense (1987) 'Notes on an alternative model: neither/nor', in M. Davies, M. Marable, P. Pfeil and M. Sprinker (eds) *The Year Left 2*, London: Verso.
Spivak, Gayatri (1987) *In Other Worlds*, London: Methuen.
—— (1989) 'The political economy of women: as seen by a literary critic', in E. Weed (ed.) *Coming To Terms*, London: Routledge & Kegan Paul.
Steedman, Carolyn (1986) *Landscape for a Good Woman*, London: Virago.
Vance, Carol (ed.) (1984) *Pleasure and Danger*, London: Routledge & Kegan Paul.
Walker, Alice (1982) *The Color Purple*, New York: Harcourt Brace Jovanovich.
—— (1984) *In Search of our Mothers' Gardens*, London: Women's Press.
—— (1989) *The Temple of my Familiar*, London: Women's Press.
Williams, J., Cocking, J. and Davies, L. (1989) *A Review of Equal Opportunity Policies in Higher Education*, London: Commission for Racial Equality.
Woolf, Virginia (1939) *Three Guineas*, London: Hogarth Press.

8

HAVING YOUR ASSUMPTIONS QUESTIONED
A guide to the 'theory guides'

Patrick Parrinder

Professor Terence Hawkes (who is well informed in these matters) has recently stated that ' "Critical theory" has become something that academics need to know about in order to get jobs and move about in the world' (Hawkes 1991: 3). If academics need to know about theory, so do their students. The 'theory market' in academic publishing aims to meet the needs of both groups through the provision of 'readers', 'reader's guides' and the like, recycling the material that initially appears in the form of monographs, journal articles and collections of essays, and translations mainly from the French. So significant has the textbook market in theory become that virtually any book on literary criticism with the words 'theory' and 'introduction' in its title is now considered to be eminently saleable. Most readers and students of theory make use of these books, and many encounter theoretical writing only through the medium of anthologies and surveys. It is customary to regard these utilitarian textbooks as wholly marginal to the enterprise of literary theory. But – to invoke one of the clichés or favourite tropes of the genre with which I am concerned in this essay – such assumptions are questionable and need to be challenged. The authors of guides to literary theory tend to make very modest claims for their own work, yet the same authors frequently question the privileging of authorial statements. Many of the theory guides also denigrate the notion of a literary canon – the canon is frequently portrayed as a merely ideological construction – and this should lead us in turn to question the canon of theory. Whose interests does it serve, we may ask, to maintain the all-pervading conventional distinction between the high theoretician and the lowly introducer of theory?

What I wish to suggest is that, in assessing the state of theory today, the reader's guides are, or should be, prime exhibits. We can learn things from them that we should not find out simply by studying prestigious examples of 'high' theory. This is not only because the guides are more widely read. They play a large part in constructing the field or discipline of literary theory, by selecting, bringing together and synthesising different theories; and, besides, the process of introducing theory, like that of translation, has a time-honoured place in theory production. Aristotle's *Poetics* and Saussure's *Course in General Linguistics* are only two instances of what, following the example of another high theorist, we might call the genre of the introductory lecture. Theory has entered recent Anglo-American literary criticism largely through the medium of translations of, and introductions to, existing European theories and theorists. The role of introductions to structuralism and poststructuralism, from the Cambridge pamphlet *Signs of the Times: Introductory Readings in Textual Semiotics* (1971), through Jonathan Culler's *Structuralist Poetics* (1975), to some of the volumes in the New Accents series inaugurated in 1977 by Terence Hawkes, is part of the intellectual history of the 1970s in the English-speaking world.

Hawkes's general preface to the highly influential New Accents series begins not merely with the questioning but the undermining of assumptions: 'the erosion of the assumptions and presuppositions that support the literary disciplines in their conventional form has proved fundamental'. Each volume in the series would offer an 'objective exposition of significant developments in its field up to the present' (some assumptions remain uneroded in that statement, one might think), together with an account of its author's own views and a bibliographic guide to further study (Hawkes 1977: 7–8). About thirty titles are currently (early 1993) in print, so that to follow up all the hints they offer for further study would be extraordinarily demanding. By the early 1980s a different kind of 'reader's guide' was born – the comprehensive one-volume survey of literary theory, beginning with the first edition of Ann Jefferson and David Robey's *Modern Literary Theory: A Comparative Introduction* (1982), and achieving runaway success in the following year with Terry Eagleton's *Literary Theory: An Introduction*. In the present chapter I compare these texts with a set of more recent books aimed, despite individual differences, at much the same market. In rough order of publication these are Raman Selden's *A Reader's Guide to Contemporary Literary Theory* (1985), Jeremy Hawthorn's *Unlocking the Text: Fundamental Issues in Literary Theory* (1987), G. Douglas Atkins and Laura Morrow's *Contemporary Literary Theory* (1989), David Birch's *Language, Literature and Critical Practice: Ways of Analysing Text* (Interface series, 1989), Raman Selden's *Practising Theory and Reading Literature: An Introduction* (1989), Alan Durant and Nigel Fabb's *Literary Studies in Action* (Interface series, 1990), K.M. Newton's *Interpreting the Text: A Critical Introduction to the Theory and Practice of Literary Interpretation* (1990), and Roger Webster's *Studying Literary Theory: An Introduction* (1990). Not listed here are the numerous current 'readers' in literary theory – such as Peter Barry's *Issues in Contemporary Critical Theory: A Casebook* (1987) and K.M. Newton's *Twentieth-Century Literary Theory: A Reader* (1988) – although some of them closely resemble the guides in aims and structure.

THE POLITICS OF THEORY GUIDES

The guides listed vary considerably – for example, some of them are multi-authored and others have a single author – but a significant number of them follow the example of Eagleton's *Literary Theory* in being polemical, British and short.[1] The implications of the polemical and often dogmatic nature of these texts will be considered later. We might start, however by asking whether there is a relationship between the authors' embattled stance and the presumed British origins of both authors and readers. Several of the books refer to the 'theoryless' state of literary studies in Britain (Jefferson and Robey 1986: 79; Barry 1987: 8), while others stress the 'active' and 'practical' nature of the theories they describe, thus going some way to meet their supposedly 'theoryless' readers. Hawthorn's book, which is intellectually at variance with most of the other guides, carries a publisher's blurb stating that 'The author has attempted to avoid all unnecessary jargon, and the book is clearly written and undogmatic in tone' (Hawthorn 1987). (Whether undogmatic or not, it is certainly argumentative.)

To some extent one can explain the tendentiousness of these

books by the fact that the authors are British academics accustomed to haranguing docile audiences of undergraduate literary specialists. Such audiences, unlike those in the American graduate schools, are probably quite willing to agree with a lecturer or author who accuses them of being insular and intellectually amateurish. The American editors of *Contemporary Literary Theory*, by contrast, do not seem to envisage the possibility of directly addressing an undergraduate readership on theoretical matters at all:

> If even the specialists find the array of competing theories bewildering, what of the 'general reader', who often is a teacher at the college and university level? And even worse, what of the student, graduate or undergraduate, confronted with so many theoretical positions, strategies, and terminologies, some of them (at least) certain to appear alien if not alienating, many being foreign imports?
>
> (Atkins and Morrow 1989: viii)

At least it might be claimed the British are by now more open to 'foreign imports' of theory than American students are held to be.

However, literary-critical polemic has deep roots in British intellectual life. Some of the guides manage to hit a note of self-righteous abrasiveness strongly reminiscent of the very orthodoxy ('Leavisism') that they claim to be attacking. As for the questioning of conventional assumptions, this can seem to echo the sort of adversarial shadow-boxing which characterises British politics, much of it based on tactics first learned in the school debating society. At parliamentary 'Question Time' (but the same format is loosely imitated in television and radio programmes, and in the courts) the leader of the Opposition has the task, week in, week out, of ridiculing the policies of the government of the day by means of an interrogative method. Nothing, or very little, is changed by this constant questioning of the ruling party's assumptions; but all oppositions dream of the mighty Change when they will suddenly become the government. Much remains unchanged when that happens, too. Literary theory in Britain has often seemed content with such an institutionalised oppositional stance. Before the Change comes, it keeps the argument going by means of questions designed to entertain the public and to make the other side sound pretty silly. The process is too often dignified by the notion of an exemplary 'politics of theory'.

British politicians assume that members of the public are already familiar with the forms and conventions of political debate; if not, they will soon pick them up. The readers addressed by the theory guides are likewise not complete novices in literary matters. An author who announces the end of readerly innocence and the need to overturn 'common sense' notions about literature takes it for granted that the reader is in some position to respond. Selden, for example, invites his readers to 'make the transition from an untheoretised set of mainly post-Romantic assumptions to a mainly poststructuralist (or even postmodern) set'. This will 'liberate readers from hidebound and unexamined critical conventions' (Selden 1989: 13). Such a liberation might need to proceed cautiously, however, and the blurb to Webster's *Studying Literary Theory* describes it as 'carefully linking theoretical concepts to more traditional terms to ensure that the areas discussed are not wholly unfamiliar territory' (Webster 1990). Jeremy Hawthorn sets out to show the 'relevance of studying theory, especially to students nervous of or sceptical about [it]' (Hawthorn 1987: 2).

This assumption of prior familiarity with conventional literary ideas leads to a structure of argument based on negations. 'Literature is not (as you may have thought, and have most likely been told) A – it is B': that is the repeated message of the theory guides. Once we have been liberated by seeing literature as B, we will need for certain purposes to go on seeing it as A as well, at least if we are to go on responding to the theory guide's rhetoric. A stands for the conventional orthodoxy, usually identified with Leavisism or the New Criticism, which the reader is expected to have consciously or unconsciously absorbed. For example, Webster polemicises against 'traditional modes of criticism', which he regards as 'unscientific', 'pre-theoretical' and based on 'Anglo-American empiricism' (Webster 1990: 11, 13, 51). Birch attacks 'intrinsic criticism' and its 'moral orthodoxies', though he concedes that intrinsic criticism is 'something of a convenient fiction' (Birch 1989: 2, 63). Selden still more candidly admits to using New Criticism as a 'typical stalking-horse of more recent theories' (Selden 1989: 126).

It goes without saying that Leavisism and New Criticism are

over-simplified and sometimes misrepresented in the process of being reduced to an orthodoxy in this way. While Atkins and Morrow, Hawthorn, and Jefferson and Robey give conscientious and fair-minded accounts, some of the other guides are guilty of distortions and elementary mistakes (it would be invidious to give examples). In any case, Thomas Kuhn has influentially argued in *The Structure of Scientific Revolutions* that the rewriting and miswriting of the history of the discipline concerned is an inevitable and even a positive feature of scientific development. Kuhn argues that the adoption of a new 'paradigm' (defined as a fruitful and authoritative model of cognitive practice) is the central event of a scientific revolution, and he sums up the spirit of the new textbooks produced in the aftermath of a paradigm change by quoting A.N. Whitehead's dictum that 'A science that hesitates to forget its founders is lost' (Kuhn 1970: 138).

However uncomfortable that may be as a watchword applied to disciplines such as literary studies, it suggests we should not quibble too much over the theory guides' distortion of the past. A much more significant point is that these guides are very different from the post-revolutionary textbooks described by Kuhn, even though they often claim to be the embodiments of a new paradigm in literary theory. In fact, the very insistence with which an author such as Raman Selden announces that a 'paradigm shift' has taken place makes that claim suspect. Theory is rather obviously not (or, its proponents might say, not yet) the new 'common sense', since if it were it would require much blander textbooks. Nicholas Tredell has written that the notion of a 'Copernican revolution' leading to a new literary-theoretical paradigm implies an 'unequivocal breakthrough which only ignorance and reactionary prejudice can deny. It depends for its effect on the echoes of an almost Victorian faith in science as an authoritative mode of knowledge' (Tredell 1987: 97). But this is a faith and an epistemology that most introductions to contemporary theory set out to debunk.

In Kuhn's model of the history of a scientific discipline, the emergence of new theories is preceded by a 'period of pronounced professional insecurity' (Kuhn 1970: 67-8). That sounds like the period through which literary studies is currently passing. Once the discipline has regrouped around a new paradigm, however, the textbooks it needs are ones which 'render revolutions invisible'. 'From the beginning of the scientific enterprise, a textbook presentation implies, scientists have striven for the particular objectives that are embodied in today's paradigms' (ibid.: 140). Writing about the natural sciences rather than the humanities, Kuhn evidently fails to conceive of textbooks which openly present their discipline as one riven by conflicts, and which themselves seem designed to function as weapons in the 'theory wars'.

THE CHOICE OF THEORIES

All the guides that I am considering acknowledge the ostensible pluralism of contemporary literary theory. For some, this reflects the confusion of a period preceding a paradigm shift; these books leave us in no doubt as to which of the contending paradigms they hope will emerge. Others view contemporary pluralism as a form of diversity within the wider unity of a paradigm shift that has already taken place. Jefferson and Robey distinguish their own 'relativistic' position from this kind of pluralism: relativists (according to their definition) argue that given an informed, comparative study of the conflicting theories, certain choices must ultimately be made (Jefferson and Robey 1986: 19). At least a mild form of relativism, as opposed to pluralism, is inherent in the very act of producing a reader's guide. K.M. Newton, a professed pluralist, agrees that the state of contemporary interpretation is one of a 'power struggle between critical modes striving for dominance' (Newton 1990: vii) and, since the author of a guide must select and reinterpret the theories to be introduced to students, all such authors participate in this power struggle. Selden's *Reader's Guide* disavows the aim of giving a 'comprehensive picture' of modern critical theory, concentrating instead on the 'most challenging and prominent trends' (Selden 1985: 4–5). Atkins and Morrow assert that, even among the theories they choose to discuss, there are major discrepancies in 'conceptual rigour and consistency, power, self-consciousness, and value for literary studies' (Atkins and Morrow 1989: ix). Eagleton argues that the criterion of value should be the theory's ability to 'contribute to the strategic goal of human emancipation, the production of "better people" through the socialist transformation of society'

(Eagleton 1983: 211). Birch piously affirms that 'all academic work should be committed to influencing the better development and improving the rights of human beings' (Birch 1989: 30). (This is the same critic who ridiculed the 'moral orthodoxies' of earlier criticism.) And Selden urges that theory should be judged by the depth of its commitment to 'unravelling the entire project of Western "bourgeois" humanism' – in other words, by its 'subversive' power (Selden 1989: 6, 8).

Though there is a thread of political power-worship running through these judgements, the guides display a degree of unanimity in their choice of theories which is not wholly explained by their official statements about what makes a good or an important theory. Jefferson and Robey, who were the first in the field, decided to 'focus firmly on what [they believed] to be the most important' theories and categories of theory, on ideas that 'do most to illuminate, either by clarification or by opposition, established critical and scholarly practice' (Jefferson and Robey 1986: 20). Subsequent guides make this statement sound distinctly conservative, yet the canon or shopping-list of theories set out by Jefferson and Robey is paralleled (with some significant changes) in most of their successors. Eagleton's *Literary Theory* avoids discussion of Marxism and feminism for the somewhat idiosyncratic reason that these are the kinds of theory he wholeheartedly endorses. (He had, however, earlier written a valuable separate introduction to Marxist literary theory.) Eagleton also focuses on hermeneutics and interpretative theory, an innovation that is perhaps reflected in the addition of a chapter on 'Reading and interpretation' – together with one on 'Feminist literary criticism' – in the second (1986) edition of Jefferson and Robey. Selden's brief 1985 *Reader's Guide* omits New Criticism, but the scope of its six chapters closely resembles Jefferson and Robey's second edition. Selden's most notable omission is of any separate treatment of psychoanalytic theory – he brings together psychoanalysis, semiotics, deconstruction and discourse theory in a single chapter on poststructuralism. The guides published up to and including 1990 incorporate much the same mixture; none of them, for example, takes much notice of postmodernist theory.

Myth criticism, recent genre theory (including the theory of science fiction and fantasy), and theories of culture and the media are normally excluded from these books, despite their impact on contemporary literary studies. Other kinds of theory may be treated in an unduly narrow way; for example, Selden discusses narratology in an exclusively structuralist context. In some cases there is an explicit recycling of material from one guide to another. Selden's *Practising Theory and Reading Literature* begins with a sketch of contemporary theory using satirical quotations from David Lodge's novel *Small World*; later the joke wears thin when the author offers a critique of New Criticism (Selden 1989: 26–9) virtually identical with Eagleton's six years earlier.

AFTER THE NEW CRITICISM

Some of the books under consideration might be called shopper's guides or shelf-guides, since their basic mode of procedure is that of selective listing or field-coverage. Atkins and Morrow, Eagleton, Jefferson and Robey, Newton, and both texts by Selden come under this heading. The overall plan of the shelf-guides tends to follow an assumed chronology charting the 'advent' or 'influx' of the different kinds of theory. By contrast, the guides by Birch, Durant and Fabb, Hawthorn, and Webster set out to reconstruct the spectrum of literary theory from first principles. While the shelf-guides had no obvious precedent before 1982 (apart from the separate volumes of the New Accents series), the 'first principles' guides have a major New Critical precursor in René Wellek and Austin Warren's *Theory of Literature* (first edition 1949). To Hawthorn (though not, I suspect, to many of the authors I am considering) *Theory of Literature* is 'still an excellent introductory study' (Hawthorn 1987: 130). To compare it with the current guides is a revealing exercise. Wellek and Warren were able to declare, in 1949, that theirs was a book without parallel in the English language. They anticipated that American scholars of that time might regard an attempt to formulate the basic assumptions of literary study as 'presumptuous', 'grandiose' and even 'unscholarly'. At the same time, they wrote as partisans of and not as refugees from the Anglo-American critical tradition. How times change. Wellek and Warren were able to assert with some pride that, though their project had German and Russian precedents, they were 'not eclectic like the Germans or doctrinaire like the Russian' (Wellek and Warren 1980: 7).

Theory of Literature is based on a fusion of New Critical principles with Russian Formalist concepts such as the 'aesthetic function' and the 'dominant'. After some preliminary chapters the book is divided into two main sections, on the 'Extrinsic' and the 'Intrinsic' study of literature respectively. The latter section is more than twice as long as its counterpart. Not only has the focus shifted from the intrinsic to the extrinsic in the more recent guides, but *Theory of Literature* partly justifies Birch's contention that the whole New Critical movement was one of propaganda for intrinsic criticism. Birch, as we shall see, vehemently rejects intrinsic criticism even though his primary orientation is towards linguistics. We may divide the theory guides in general into those asserting a degree of continuity with older versions of literary theory, and those proclaiming a complete break with it. Jefferson and Robey begin by declaring that most modern literary theorists are 'conscious of belonging to a tradition that goes back at least as far as Plato and Aristotle' (Jefferson and Robey 1986: 7). Later, in even more traditionalist vein, they assert that 'we are not suggesting that theory should ever replace criticism' (ibid.: 21). Hawthorn takes a similar line. Continuity with earlier theory could probably be measured by the prominence given in a contemporary textbook to the intrinsic study of literature, and by the presence or absence of such key terms as allegory, ambiguity, analysis, diction, genre, irony, mode, plot, rhetoric, symbolism and value. Some of the guides strongly imply that earlier critics and theorists concerned with these matters were wasting their time.

It may be argued, however, that New Criticism, rather than more recent developments, represented the decisive break in the continuity of literary theory. Eagleton and Webster stress the institutional transformation of literary studies at the beginning of the twentieth century, and Webster goes so far as to describe the New Critical shift from biographical to textual analysis as a 'critical Copernican revolution' (Webster 1990: 24). Both authors, however, think that this revolution either has been or ought to be displaced by the subsequent revolution that they themselves champion. K.M. Newton's *Interpreting the Text* identifies the New Critics as the forerunners of the interpretative movement that Newton values most in contemporary criticism: unlike Johnson, Arnold, and Leavis, Newton writes, New Critical theory led to a 'virtual identification of criticism with interpretation' (Newton 1990: 16). On the other hand, Birch, Durant and Fabb, and Selden join Eagleton and Webster in trying to bury New Criticism. Selden puts it very forthrightly: 'The main purpose of this book is to introduce [the] radical forms of theory and some of their antecedents, and to show their effects on reading practice. To put it simply, we can and must learn to *read differently'* (Selden 1989: 4; original emphasis). This desire to read differently implies a radical reformulation of the basic problematics of literary study. For Wellek and Warren, the fundamental problem was the need to combine recognition of the individuality of poetic art with the search for generalised historical laws (Wellek and Warren 1980: 17–19). But this ceases to be a problem for contemporary theories committed, in Selden's words, to unravelling Western humanism by 'questioning notions such as the autonomy of essential human values' (Selden 1989: 6). Instead, we might say, the central problem becomes the so-called death of literature and of its study, to which Eagleton looks forward with relish (Eagleton 1983: 217), though Selden draws back from this perspective in favour of a much vaguer commitment to a 'radical change of focus' (Selden 1989: 5, 169).[2]

PEDAGOGIC CLICHÉS

If the authors of theory guides are serious about questioning our inherited notions then they should, of course, be prepared to question the conventions of the introductory textbook itself. Wellek and Warren were apprehensive that every literary specialist would 'unavoidably be dissatisfied with [their] account of his specialty' (Wellek and Warren 1980: 7). Contemporary guides add to this familar disclaimer the knowledge that some of the most admired modern theories are self-consciously hostile to abstraction and popularisation. Ann Jefferson concludes a chapter on structuralism and post-structuralism with the observation that 'To obey the rules of the genre of the "introductory account", to use the rhetoric of exposition is, in a sense, necessarily to betray the most interesting insights of "Derrida" ' (Jefferson and Robey 1986: 119).

Even a caveat like this is not as cautious and self-critical as it might be, besides being a virtual afterthought. What is betrayal 'in a sense', and how does it differ from ordinary betrayal? What is meant by an 'insight', in this context? (The late J.C.T. Oates, a scholar and bibliographer of the old school, used to claim that literary studies had been ruined by the New Criticism with its pursuit of textual 'insights'.)

Two of the guides under consideration – Eagleton's *Literary Theory* and Durant and Fabb's *Literary Studies in Action* – seem to stand aside from the assumptions of the introductory account in certain ways, and I shall return to them. The other guides are standard pedagogic narratives exhibiting conventional academic anxieties and, in one or two cases, indulging extravagantly in pedagogic cliché. The vocabulary of 'questioning', 'challenging' and 'problematising' soon becomes a cliché, as the reader of this chapter may have noticed. Selden declares that 'all literary students now need to take on board the intellectual challenge of modern theories' (Selden 1989: 13) – perhaps this is the notion of theory as a lifeboat, which we should take on board but need not rush into. Hawthorn and Birch explore the lower reaches of pedagogic cliché, with innumerable paragraphs which begin by highlighting points worth making, comments that are in order, crucial notions and important ways of thinking.

Of all these authors, Birch – a proponent of 'critical linguistics', who wants to abolish traditional literary studies in favour of a 'text-based discourse-based approach to language' (Birch 1989: 168) – is the least effective in communicating his message. His style is monotonous, slipshod and wearisome. Not only is an abundance of pedagogic cliché the sign of a bad textbook, but the use of such clichés to expound deconstructionist views, such as those advocated in Birch's opening chapter, makes the theorist willy-nilly his own worst enemy. If what he says is 'true', then it should not have been said in that way. (In fact I believe this is part of the significance of introductory accounts, for in them the fault-lines of theory are clearly exposed.) Faced, for example, with a barrage of professions of faith, 'crucial points' and peremptory assertions, it seems a little perverse to be told that the notions of authorial meaning, textual relevance and stable interpretation are now obsolete.

'No knowledge is ever fixed for ever', writes Birch (ibid.: 16), offering an epigrammatic example of the statement that unknowingly deconstructs itself. Birch knows what deconstruction means and why it is so important. 'Central to the deconstructionist enterprise is a questioning of the underlying assumptions of a text' (ibid.: 11). In a different context he explains that the notion of the 'centre' is a 'very important one in intrinsic criticism' – Eliot's *Four Quartets* are rather peculiarly brought in as evidence – and that such a notion is objectionable because it 'closes off all possibility of other meanings, other readings' (ibid.: 83). That is the problem with pedagogic discourse. The guides frequently make 'challenging' and 'questioning' theories sound like new forms of positivism. Some of the blame must lie with the theories themselves, since a theory which cannot be expounded without being betrayed is at best an intellectual halfway house and at worst an imposture. Equally, the difficulties may result from the attempts of the theory guides to synthesise different theories and to combine them together into a single 'revolutionary' paradigm or world-view.

Some of our authors are anxious to reconcile varieties of deconstructionism with Marxism and feminism. Webster, for example, affirms his commitment to the multiplicity and uncertainty of meanings (which may be an odd thing to be 'committed' to), but he is also convinced that 'Literary values and literary criticism always have a specific relation to class' (Webster 1990: 57). That which is specific can be specified, rather than being left in uncertainty, one might have thought. Birch explains sententiously that we live in a world which is 'culturally, socially and institutionally determined', but which is also 'messy, noisy, and full of disturbances, surprises, and instability' (Birch 1989: 2). However recognisable this description may be, it does not inspire theoretical confidence. Birch concludes that 'Analysing text is therefore about interpreting language as meaningful action' (ibid.: 168), though on his premises particular instances of language might equally appear as meaningless or passive. Since he states that 'My critical position – my analysis – is a political act, as indeed *all* criticism is' (ibid.: 165; original emphasis), we might suspect that he will only follow his own arguments in the directions he feels to be politically correct. Similarly, Selden denounces Leavis's criticism for its assumption of universal moral values, but praises Marxist and feminist criticism for their honesty and intellectual courage (Selden 1989: 23). The more polemical these critics, the more indulgent they tend to be towards their own self-contradictions.

HANDLE WITH CARE

Terry Eagleton is the Bernard Shaw of literary theory, a quicksilver intelligence, a brilliant mocker and one who seldom misses an opportunity to appeal to the gallery. In *Literary Theory* he gradually discards all the theories he expounds, like so many outmoded theatrical costumes. His final chapter on 'Political criticism' denounces theory for its flight from real history and, Prospero-like, declares the whole subject to which he has devoted so many pages to be largely illusory. Whatever pedagogic devices he may have employed, he also effectively undermines the pedagogic approach by refusing to discuss the theories he most admires together with the others. At the end, he parodies the sort of theory guide which asserts the continuity of literary studies by apparently calling for the revival of the ancient discipline of rhetoric. Eagleton's is quintessentially the kind of text of which academics in more cautious days would have said, 'Handle with care' – yet it has deservedly been very widely handled, and it is incontestably the 'best buy' in the present selection.

Alan Durant and Nigel Fabb's *Literary Studies in Action* is not a textbook but a self-styled 'workbook', consisting of 111 separate exercises or 'activities' which are presented as being indeterminate and open-ended since the reader, not the authors, provides the answers. Yet, ingenious and entertaining though this is, one may find it oppressive rather than liberating in various respects. For a start, all of the exercises have a time-limit. Many of the questions are slanted so as to imply that traditional literary studies are a dead end and should give place to language study. Beginning with the innocent-sounding contention that 'the major way forward from the valuable insights of the last 30 years is towards new courses informed by theory', the authors suggest much later on that 'it is at least possible that literature may turn out to have been just a hundred-year "blip" on the screen of educational history' (Durant and Fabb 1990: 2, 207). (Note the technological metaphor.) In fact, the reading of literature is already a little displaced by this 'workbook', since if the 111 exercises were taken seriously as a teaching and learning device they would cut out a great deal of time which could otherwise be devoted to what are still known as 'primary' texts. *Literary Studies in Action*, which takes about three hours to read, contains on my calculation 76½ hours of prescribed exercise and project work. The 'texts' readers are expected to analyse are presented in the form of short extracts in the workbook itself.

THEORY AND CRITICISM

Here is an example of the kind of questioning that Durant and Fabb set out to provoke:

31. Make a note of who is paying for your studies (you, someone else, an institution, some combination, etc.)
32. Why are your studies being paid for by yourself/this person/this institution? What exactly is being bought?
(Durant and Fabb 1990: 15)

The question 'What exactly is being bought?' – however crude and simplistic it may seem when aimed at literary education as a whole – may be usefully asked of theory guides. One thing that is being bought, in some of these guides, is a deep-seated resentment against established forms of literary study. Raman Selden quotes a David Lodge fictional character as pronouncing that criticism's function is to 'wage undying war on the very concept of "literature" itself, since this concept is an agent of class oppression' (Selden 1989: 5). Selden partly dissociates himself from this, yet, as Brian Doyle has recently and approvingly written, 'the goal of much feminist, political, and critical theory might be summed up as a vision of the end of "literature" in the sense of a privileged cultural domain' (Doyle 1989: 135). Curiously enough, one does not hear much campaigning against – to take a few examples – philosophy, theory, politics, mathematics, music or even poetry as privileged cultural domains. Attempts to explain why literature is so often made the symbol of an unacceptable degree of cultural privilege do not, as a rule, go beyond the fact that high claims were made for literary study earlier in the century, within a particular critical tradition. (Yet if we substitute 'poetry' for 'literature', we will find that poetry has occupied a much contested position of cultural privilege throughout the history of human societies.) Eagleton argues tendentiously enough that it is

> difficult to spend some years studying literature in most universities and still find it pleasurable at the end: many university literature courses seem to be constructed to prevent this from happening, and those who emerge still able to enjoy literary works might be considered either heroic or perverse.
>
> (Eagleton 1983: 191)

The non-heroic and non-perverse apparently include some whose interest in the subject remains sufficiently intense for them to write guides to literary theory.

It might be felt that, if you believe in introducing students to literary theory, you must harbour some positive feelings about the rest of literature and its study. Expressions of this feeling in the theory guides tend to be rather shamefaced. David Birch is fairly typical in that his anti-literary stance does not prevent him from using the recognised literary canon as the source of nearly all his textual examples. He ends by discussing some interesting and effective verse by a contemporary Australian Aboriginal poet. Birch is happy to endorse this as 'a very powerful political statement' (Birch 1989: 157). Roger Webster denounces the 'comfortable insularity of "English" ', but he claims that theory, 'by challenging some of the dominant conventions and assumptions within traditional modes of criticism', can lead to a 'much fuller understanding of literary texts and the forms of experience generated by them' (Webster 1990: 19, 111). Hawthorn, very much at odds with his competitors, ends with a reminder of the greatness of Shakespeare and of the 'mixture of constant and changing elements that is at the core of the literary process, at the heart of literature' (Hawthorn 1987: 128–9). It is hard to say such things without invoking an even more hackneyed set of pedagogic clichés than those surveyed in this chapter. Who could deny that the bad new ideas have some uses denied to the good old ones? My reading of the theory guides leads me to challenge an assumption which is widely made, and not only by the proponents of 'political criticism': that the best guide to recommend to students is necessarily the one that you find most sensible and that you tend to agree with. It isn't so, at least in the present state of disciplinary confusion.

What of the future? Will literary theory survive as a subject in need of elementary textbooks? If the concept of literature is to be superseded, then the same must be true of literary theory. Alternatively, it seems just possible that the more traditional kind of literary studies remains lively enough to promote a return to aestheticism, reaffirming the intrinsic value of literary and, above all, poetic texts. Literary theory might then be redefined as poetics, or poetic theory, which arguably is all that literary specialists, as specialists, are really equipped to talk about. However, this unlikely scenario would involve a drastic retreat, not just from the current ambitions of literary studies but from the ambitions they have harboured throughout this century. The movement from literary to textual and cultural theory curiously lays claim to the same sorts of missionary status and discursive power that were earlier asserted by Leavisite criticism. The theory guides reflect a state of theory ashamed of, but nevertheless reluctant to lose, its origins and its accustomed place in the curriculum – a form of literary study that still attempts to win recognition as the central humanity. But this theory is dogged by the memory of its predecessor.

Theory tends to regard criticism (in the sense of the study of specific texts) as an activity properly subordinated to its own stronger and wider concerns. But it also regards criticism as the watchword of a now discredited intellectual movement – that of the literary discipline as conceived by Arnold, the New Critics and Leavis. However, what the theory guides unwittingly demonstrate is a continuing need for criticism, exploring the fault-lines and pursuing the self-contradictions to be found in theoretical statements, and asking what the current reception of these statements means and what it is worth. The relationship between theory and criticism should not be one of master and slave but a two-way process, in which not only does theory question criticism but criticism questions theory.

NOTES

1 In my judgement this generalisation applies to the cited texts by Birch, Durant and Fabb, Hawthorn, Selden (1989), and Webster.
2 Discussing Bakhtin's influence on critics seeking to recover the

radical and popular elements in high culture, Selden writes of the 'radical change of focus which this type of sociological and historical criticism affords when compared with traditional Bradleian or formalistic studies of Shakespeare'. Earlier, however, he has ridiculed Leavis's recognition of elements of 'popular idiom' in Bunyan's style (Selden 1989: 169, 21).

BIBLIOGRAPHY

Atkins, G.D. and Morrow, L. (eds) (1989) *Contemporary Literary Theory*, London: Macmillan.

Barry, P. (ed.) (1987) *Issues in Contemporary Critical Theory: A Casebook*, Basingstoke: Macmillan.

Birch, D. (1989) *Language, Literature and Critical Practice: Ways of Analysing Text*, London: Routledge.

Doyle, B. (1989) *English and Englishness*, London: Routledge.

Durant, A. and Fabb, N. (1990) *Literary Studies in Action*, London: Routledge.

Eagleton, T. (1983) *Literary Theory: An Introduction*, Oxford: Blackwell.

Hawkes, T. (1977) 'General editor's preface', in T. Hawkes *Structuralism and Semiotics*, London: Methuen.

Hawkes, T. (1991) Interview in 'Literary periodicals in focus', *Literature Matters* 9: 3.

Hawthorn, J. (1987) *Unlocking the Text: Fundamental Issues in Literary Theory*, London: Arnold.

Jefferson, A. and Robey, D. (eds) (1986) *Modern Literary Theory: A Comparative Introduction*, 2nd edn, London: Batsford.

Kuhn, T.S. (1970) *The Structure of Scientific Revolutions*, 2nd edn, Chicago: University of Chicago Press.

Newton, K.M. (ed.) (1988) *Twentieth-Century Literary Theory: A Reader*, New York: St Martin's Press.

—— (1990) *Interpreting the Text: A Critical Introduction to the Theory and Practice of Literary Interpretation*, Hemel Hempstead: Harvester Wheatsheaf.

Selden, R. (1985) *A Reader's Guide to Contemporary Literary Theory*, Brighton: Harvester.

—— (1989) *Practising Theory and Reading Literature: An Introduction*, Hemel Hempstead: Harvester Wheatsheaf.

Tredell, N. (1987) 'Euphoria (Ltd.) – the limitations of post-structuralism and deconstruction', in P. Barry (ed.) *Issues in Contemporary Critical Theory: A Casebook*, Basingstoke: Macmillan.

Webster, R. (1990) *Studying Literary Theory: An Introduction*, London: Arnold.

Wellek, R. and Warren, A. (1980) *Theory of Literature*, 3rd edn, Harmondsworth: Penguin.

9

AESTHETICS, CULTURAL STUDIES AND THE TEACHING OF ENGLISH

K.M. Newton

In a letter to the *London Review of Books*, in response to the views of critics of Shakespeare associated with 'cultural materialism', Boris Ford wrote that he could not help speculating

> when they last read one of Shakespeare's major plays as they might perhaps listen to one of Bach's unaccompanied cello sonatas or Mozart's string quintets: because they find them profoundly moving, or spiritually restoring, or simply strangely enjoyable. Or do they sit listening entranced to Bach's and Mozart's 'texts' as 'critical representations of ideological materials which disclose the conditions of their own historical existence'?
>
> Their writing doesn't convey to me the least impression that they enjoy or are moved or restored by Shakespeare. Or that they believe it is any part of their business as university teachers of literature to help their students enjoy and be moved by Shakespeare and understand how these responses arise out of the text and are controlled by the way the drama and the verse work. And ditto for Bach and Mozart, no doubt.
>
> (Ford 1990)

For Ford, clearly, Shakespeare's plays are works of art and one's fundamental response to them should be aesthetic. Cultural materialist criticism, in ignoring this aesthetic dimension, is thus anti-literary.

Boris Ford is probably best known as the editor of the *Pelican Guide to English Literature*, a series of literary critical essays on the whole range of English literature which are clearly strongly influenced by Leavis's critical principles. Explicit discussion of aesthetics is conspicuously absent from Leavis's own criticism and he notoriously rejects René Wellek's view that he should spell out and defend the basis of his critical judgements. Yet it is nevertheless apparent that there is an aesthetic dimension to Leavis's critical position, though he would, of course, deny that aesthetic value in literature could exist separately from moral and ethical concerns. It is perhaps the association of the term 'aesthetic' with the view, promoted most famously by Wilde, that art is an amoral realm that has no necessary relation with morals or ethics that makes Leavis avoid using the term. Explicit discussion of aesthetics is also seldom found in the writings of the American New Critics, who share common ground with Leavis in a number of respects, though one can find the underlying aesthetic philosophy of the New Criticism elaborated by Monroe C. Beardsley, a philosopher associated with the New Critics, in his book *Aesthetics* (1958).

Boris Ford is right to point out that recent developments in critical theory appear to have little time for aesthetics or literary value in their approach to literature, but he shows no interest in trying to understand why there should have been such a shift, nor does he seem to appreciate that this opposition to the aesthetic dimension of literature takes several forms. One obvious factor underlying such opposition is that there is clearly an ideological aspect to Leavis's and the New Critics' concept of literary value. Fundamental to the New Critics' and Leavis's emphasis on literary value is the belief that literature has the power to create a spiritual wholeness out of conflicting elements that could not be integrated by any other means: mind and body, intellect and feeling, self and world, form and content. For the New Critics and Leavis the literary text is a source of value in a disordered world and they can be seen as inheritors of Matthew Arnold's view that in a world in which religion and philosophy can no longer provide a metaphysical basis for value, poetry or literature must fill this vacuum. It is significant that the New Critics and Leavis are suspicious of the criticism of William Empson, a critic for whom a relentless analysis of language has priority over the question of literary value. For Cleanth Brooks, Empson's pursuit of ambiguity is flawed because it ignores this question:

one can make a case for richness and complexity in almost

any poem – in the poem that has not earned it as well as the poem that has . . . the mere process of spinning out a web of complexities and ambiguities is not sufficient to validate a poem. There must be a further criterion.

(Brooks 1944: 212)

Leavis is even more explicit on this point. He sees Empson's *Seven Types of Ambiguity* as a 'warning' to the critic to avoid a linguistic ingenuity dissociated from the question of value: 'Valid analytic practice is a strengthening of the sense of relevance . . . and all appropriate play of intelligence, being also an exercise of the sense of value, is controlled by an implicit concern for a total value-judgment' (Leavis 1947: 596–7).

The critic who is most opposed to what he calls 'aesthetic ideology' is the deconstructionist Paul de Man. For de Man literary study should cut itself off from both aesthetics and hermeneutics and associate itself with rhetoric and philology. He claims that 'Attention to the philological or rhetorical devices of language is not the same as aesthetic appreciation.' Literary theory is distrusted by traditional critics because it 'raises the unavoidable question whether aesthetic values can be compatible with the linguistic structures that make up the entities from which these values are derived'. Aesthetics, he argues, avoids confronting this question because it has an ideological interest in creating a fusion between literature, art, epistemology and ethics, a fusion de Man sees as motivated by a religious or metaphysical desire for some kind of spiritual union that can overcome dualism and antinomy. But for him – and here there is a clear contrast between him and the New Critics and Leavis, since he implicitly rejects Arnold's view that poetry can replace religion – the study of literary texts is incompatible with such a desire. For him the organicist aesthetic ideals which govern the thinking of the Coleridgean and Arnoldian critical tradition and which had a fundamental influence on the New Criticism and Leavis are irreconcilable with the kind of reading literary texts demand. Thus instead of literary study having its basis in aesthetics it should reject the belief that literary texts are cultural icons and view them in a much more sceptical and critical light. There should be a change in the rationale for teaching literature, 'away from standards of cultural excellence that, in the last analysis, are always based on some form of religious faith, to a principle of disbelief that is not so much scientific as it is critical, in the full philosophical sense of the term' (de Man 1982: 1,355, 1,356).

De Man's opposition to aesthetics is different in its basis from that of materialist critics, such as those Boris Ford directly attacks in his letter. The attitude of these critics is probably most clearly represented in the New Accents volume, *Re-Reading English*. For many of the critics in this volume literary criticism is not enough. It is justified only if it leads on to a critique of society which will further social change. For literary criticism to concern itself with aesthetic questions would clearly stand in the way of such an aim. Thus the concept of literary value is attacked. As Peter Widdowson puts it:

> 'Literature' is, in effect, being recognised as the construct of a criticism which, while assuming and proclaiming its 'descriptiveness', its 'disinterestedness', its ideological innocence, has so constituted Literature as to reproduce and naturalise bourgeois ideology as 'literary value'.
>
> (Widdowson 1982: 3)

The logical consequence of this is that literature itself becomes a dubious category and that texts traditionally regarded as literary cease to have any special privileges. Any text should be open to critical analysis. If one continues to analyse literary texts the aim should not be to demonstrate their aesthetic power but rather to show that these very aesthetic qualities have stood in the way of recognising the role that literature plays in constructing and reinforcing ideology. Thus materialist criticism should aim to expose the complicity of such texts with imperialism or class domination. Some contributors believe the kind of analytic techniques developed in relation to literary texts should be applied to non-literary forms of discourse. English as an academic subject should change, therefore, from being a study of literary masterpieces, judged to be such by aesthetic criteria, and become instead subsumed within cultural studies in which the focus will be on a much wider range of texts: popular works not formerly considered as worth studying in English departments, texts from virtually any type of discourse, and traditional literary texts as well – but treated as cultural artefacts and not privileged as works of art.

But looking at the present state of English studies it seems clear that it is less easy to discard the aesthetic dimension than opponents of aesthetics appear to think. With deconstructive criticism, what has taken place is not so much the rejection of the aesthetic but its redefinition. Deconstructive critics have tended to concentrate on texts of the traditional canon, though they have written also on philosophical texts and other texts that are not in conventional literary modes. They have shown greater interest in certain writers whom the New Critical tradition did not value highly, notably Shelley, though Shelley's *The Triumph of Life*, the subject of special study on the part of the Yale critics, was one of the few poems by Shelley for which Leavis had some admiration. More important is that the kind of deconstructive criticism associated with Paul de Man and J. Hillis Miller focuses on texts which, they claim, collaborate with their own deconstruction. De Man, in his seminal essay in *Blindness and Insight* in which he discusses Derrida's reading of Rousseau, an essay which had a crucial influence on the Yale School, argues that Derrida's deconstructive reading of Rousseau is contained within Rousseau's text. Thus the text embodies its own deconstruction: 'There is no need to deconstruct Rousseau; the established tradition of Rousseau interpretation, however, stands in dire need of deconstruction' (de Man 1971: 139). J. Hillis Miller has developed this de Manian approach. He claims of major literary texts: 'They have anticipated explicitly any deconstruction the critic can achieve' (Miller 1975: 31). For deconstructive critics, therefore, the greatest works are those which collaborate in the deconstructive process. Miller writes that *Middlemarch* 'pulls the rug out from under itself' and George Eliot's fiction generally 'deprives itself of its ground in history by demonstrating that ground to be a fiction too' (Miller 1974: 467). He implies that such fiction is superior in literary terms to types of fiction in which such a deconstructive dimension is absent. Though organicist aesthetic values with their basis in an achieved harmony and unity that reconciles oppositions and conflicts are rejected by deconstructionist criticism, they are replaced by a different conception of literary value which does not seriously alter the traditional literary canon even though it does not seek to demonstrate unity or reconciliation; as Hillis Miller puts it, deconstructive criticism is not concerned with organic unity but with 'heterogeneity of form', the 'oddnesses' in literary texts that subvert the text's effort to achieve such unity (Miller 1982: 5).

Materialist criticism on the surface seems to break more radically with literary value. Unlike deconstructionist criticism with its implicit belief in a hierarchy of discourses which preserves the special status of literature or the literary, it claims that literary texts should not be regarded as privileged and that they should not be treated as intrinsically superior to other types of text. The traditional practice of merely using non-literary texts as a means of illuminating the literary text is condemned. But in practice new historicist and cultural materialist criticism focuses predominantly on literary texts that are part of the traditional canon. It is hard to think of any critical study that devotes its attention solely to such forms of discourse as government reports, as one of the contributors to *Re-Reading English* advocates (Widdowson 1982: 164–78).

The leading new historicist critic, Stephen Greenblatt, has specialised in employing literary critical forms of analysis in relation to non-literary texts, but he almost invariably goes on to deal with traditional literary texts at much greater length. In *Renaissance Self-Fashioning*, for example, he discusses a text concerned with mining for gold in Central America before interpreting *Othello*. The non-literary text is not treated as secondary in any intrinsic sense to the literary text; both are viewed as cultural artefacts. His stated aim in that book is to create 'a more cultural or anthropological criticism' that is 'intent upon understanding literature as a part of the system of signs that constitutes a given culture'. But what emerges from his book is that the literary texts he discusses clearly require a much more complex analysis than non-literary texts. Though Greenblatt sees himself as breaking from traditional aesthetically based criticism, he still regards himself as a literary critic primarily and believes literary texts have a special value: 'The literary text remains the central object of my attention in this study of self-fashioning in part because . . . great art is an extraordinarily sensitive register of the complex struggles and harmonies of culture' (Greenblatt 1980: 4, 5). Catherine Belsey, a critic associated both with British poststructuralism and with cultural criticism, has argued recently that though English studies should move towards cultural studies and reject the idea that it is the study of masterpieces, nevertheless traditional literary texts should not be discarded in this process: 'there is no special political or pedagogical merit in severing all ties with the texts the institution of English has done its best to make its own' (Belsey 1989: 159).[1]

Though critics such as those that Boris Ford castigates may not write about Shakespeare's plays in a manner which indicates that they respond aesthetically to such works, this is not unusual in criticism. The same could be said about scholarly or textual critics. The more important question is whether such criticism is of relevance to those whose interests in reading Shakespeare are traditionally literary. It seems to me that the best of such critics produce insights into the plays that can enhance any reader's appreciation. Only those who adhere to the most extreme aestheticism of a Wildean type would deny this. Greenblatt is surely a major critic by any standards, one who constantly illuminates the texts he writes about, and in much cultural materialist criticism, though political and social analysis is primary, the critic also endeavours to produce a reading which is more persuasive than conventional readings in relation to literary structure. Thus, though Alan Sinfield, in an essay on *Macbeth*, sees himself as writing 'an oppositional criticism' whose 'task is to work across the grain of customary assumptions and, if necessary, across the grain of the text, as it is customarily perceived' (Sinfield 1986: 75), he also claims that his reading of the play, which discusses it in relation to the writings of George Buchanan, is not imposed on the text. In effect it is an attempt to produce a more convincing reading of the play in structural terms than traditional interpretations:

> the Buchanan disturbance *is in the play*, and inevitably so. Even if we believe that Shakespeare was trying to smooth over difficulties in Absolutist ideology, to do this significantly he must deal with the issues which resist convenient inclusion. Those issues must be brought into visibility in order that they can be handled, and once exposed they are available for the reader or audience to seize and focus upon, as an alternative to the more complacent reading.
>
> (Sinfield 1986: 71–2; original emphasis)

Sinfield's focusing on the play's relation to political and ideological conflicts in Shakespeare's own time leads into the question of its literary structure; his reading is no more divorced from aesthetic considerations than discussions which look at the play in relation to the Elizabethan world picture or the great chain of being.

An interesting shift can be discerned in Terry Eagleton's view of the aesthetic. In his book *Literary Theory: An Introduction* he criticised the concept of the aesthetic as vigorously as de Man, though from a different perspective: 'The assumption that there was an unchanging object known as "art", or an isolatable experience called "beauty" or the "aesthetic", was largely a product of the very alienation of art from social life which we have already touched on' (Eagleton 1983: 21). However, in his more recent book, *The Ideology of the Aesthetic*, though critical of how the aesthetic as a category has been used to try to create a realm outside the social and political, he is opposed to discarding it entirely. It would be a mistake to hand it over to political conservatives: 'Truth, morality and beauty are too important to be handed contemptuously over to the political enemy' (Eagleton 1990: 372). Though sympathetic to Paul de Man's 'demystification of the idea of the aesthetic', he believes that de Man's position is a reaction to his dubious political past and that he 'is led to suppress the potentially positive dimensions of the aesthetic in a way which perpetuates, if now in a wholly new style, his earlier hostility to an emancipatory politics' (ibid.: 10). Eagleton recognises the dangers of the aesthetic, especially when conceived in terms of disinterested and timeless contemplation, but he also believes it can potentially promote liberation:

> The aesthetic is at once . . . the very secret prototype of human subjectivity in early capitalist society, and a vision of human energies as radical ends in themselves which is the implacable enemy of all dominative or instrumentalist thought. It signifies a creative turn to the sensuous body, as well as an inscribing of that body with a subtly oppressive law; it represents on the one hand a liberatory concern with concrete particularity, and on the other a specious form of universalism.
>
> (ibid.: 9)

Though he does not discuss what his positive conception of the aesthetic might mean in relation to literature, Eagleton's view does imply that the literary as a category should be retained, which contrasts with the position he takes in *Literary Theory: An Introduction*, namely, that English as an academic subject should devote itself to the analysis of discursive practices, with aesthetic considerations having little or no place. In other words it would appear to be necessary to retain the concept of literary or aesthetic value, though such value may be determined on a different basis from that of traditional criticism.

In Britain – at least in most of the older universities; the situation may be different in the new universities or former polytechnics of which I have no direct knowledge – English departments have been only marginally affected by the conflict between defenders of the traditional canon with its basis in literary value and those who advocate cultural studies. The traditional canon remains largely in place, with certain modifications such as the increased representation of women's writing, and debate has centred on how literary texts should be studied. In American universities, however, the canon has been under much more serious attack. The increasing participation in higher education of students from non-European ethnic backgrounds and the greater power of feminism have led to the canon being vigorously attacked for the fact that it largely consists of works by white men of European cultural background. Thus extremists have argued that the traditional canon should be rejected in favour of syllabuses made up only of women's writing or Black writing. However, it is doubtful even in this situation if aesthetic considerations have been abandoned. Rather than the rejection in principle of the concept of a canon made up of texts regarded as having literary merit, what is being advocated is the creation of alternative canons. For social and political reasons the traditional canon may be set aside, but literary value is still not discarded; rather it operates within restricted categories, such as women's writing or Black writing. For example, Henry Louis Gates, probably the leading Black literary theorist, emphasises the existence of a Black literary tradition and writes that the role of Black critics should be to

> respect the integrity of the separate traditions embodied
> in the black work of art, by bringing to bear upon the
> explication of its meanings all of the attention to language

that we may learn from several developments in contemporary theory.

(Gates 1989: 334)

Even in America, then, one does not seem close to a situation in
which English studies will abandon aesthetic considerations
totally and draw up a syllabus on entirely different principles.

If even supporters of cultural studies opposed to traditional
literary study within English departments continue to accept
literary value based on aesthetic considerations in one form or
another, could one therefore go to the other extreme and argue
not only that the aesthetic should be seen as fundamental to
English studies as a discipline but also that the cultural, the
social, the textual or the political are essentially extraneous to
literary study? In order to investigate whether such a position
is tenable I shall consider Stein Haugom Olsen's book, *The End of
Literary Theory*. Olsen, a critic with a background in analytic
philosophy, seeks to provide a coherent defence and justification of literary aesthetics and attacks alternative literary
approaches which reject or discard the aesthetic. His own
critical position is predominantly that of the later New
Criticism; as he puts it in his earlier book, *The Structure of Literary
Understanding*, 'all the identifiable parts of a literary work should
be artistically relevant . . . Ideally, a text which is construed as a
literary work can be segmented completely so that no part of
the text is resistant to interpretation' (Olsen 1978: 146)

Olsen attacks those who see literature in terms of ideology or
politics or textuality on the grounds that literary works, which
he believes are intrinsically different from other texts, are
constituted by aesthetic features which cannot be incorporated
within political or textual categories. He argues that a distinction must be made between textual and aesthetic features. All
texts possess textual features which will be recognised by any
linguistically competent reader, but, he claims, aesthetic
features cannot be reduced to textual terms, since they are
defined institutionally. Olsen attempts to shift the focus from
literature as text and thus part of textuality in general, to
literature as a social practice in which certain conventions of
reading and interpretation govern the identification of aesthetic features. Though there may be disagreement about what
should be included in the literary canon or about questions of

interpretation, this is not important as long as there is general agreement about the existence of such a canon, that those works included in it have cultural value and that they respond to a certain type of reading. The aim of criticism is to be illuminating about such works and thus to enhance aesthetic appreciation of them. A reader's response to a literary work is, he writes, 'correctly described as an *imaginative reconstruction* of its literary aesthetic features' (Olsen 1987: 16; original emphasis). The essential difference between an aesthetic approach and a theoretical one is that the former denies that the literary work can be 'defined through a set of textual features, be they relational, textural, or structural. The literary work is an irreducible entity whose literary features are grasped only in appreciation' (ibid.: 207). For such aesthetic appreciation to take place, the reader must go beyond the textual material of the work in order to make thematic or structural connections which can imbue any particular element in a literary work with significance and interest. Such connections, Olsen claims, can be apprehended only by the reader who understands the text as a literary work.

It seems to me that Olsen's attempt to construct a literary aesthetics which cuts the literary text off from anything outside the sphere of the aesthetic is as one-sided as attempts to deny that aesthetics have any relevance in literary study. Both literature and literary criticism cannot be rigidly pinned down in this way, since they are made up of elements which are diverse by their very nature. Olsen's attempt to impose a coherence based only on aesthetic considerations on literary study inevitably breaks down. For example, he makes a comparison between the practice of literary criticism and chess. In both, he claims, institutional rules govern procedures. A move in chess can be understood only if it is seen 'as contributing to the institutionally defined purpose of the game, that of attempting to win' (ibid.: 27). One is therefore not playing chess unless one has such a purpose, just as one is not reading a literary text in any proper sense unless one is reading it in terms of literary aesthetics. Yet it is easy to imagine circumstances in which one may play chess, make all the correct moves, but have no intention of winning – if, for instance, one is playing against someone, such as a child, who would be upset at losing. I see no reason why it should be claimed that one is not playing chess in such circumstances.

Similarly, literary texts can be read by people with little or no interest in aesthetic appreciation as Olsen conceives it, but this need not mean that the purposes that motivate them to read are invalid or that their responses will be of no literary interest. For instance, a reader may be a philosopher whose interest is in finding philosophical significance in works of a fictional nature. Of course, such an interest could be served by works which have no merit judged by literary aesthetic criteria, but I feel sure that a reader with philosophical interests would soon find that his or her purposes were better served by Jane Austen, George Eliot or Proust than by Jeffrey Archer or Barbara Cartland. Such a reader's interpretations might be of considerable critical interest, as a philosophical analysis could reveal that the work of the former group of writers engages with and challenges the philosophical or ideological expectations of the reader whereas the work of the latter novelists does not constitute any such challenge. For the literary critic, this would be relevant to the question of aesthetic value and would show that there was common ground with the philosophical reader even though the latter may be quite uninterested in aesthetic considerations.

Olsen sees aesthetic features as intrinsic to those texts which are categorised as literature, but when one considers the conventional literary canon it is plain that no clear-cut separation between the aesthetic and the historical is possible. Many texts are included in the literary canon and thus read in aesthetic terms because they are regarded by the literary community as historically important on the grounds of having made some stylistic or generic innovation, or they may be the only works of a particular period to have survived. In contrast, there are texts which may possess considerable aesthetic interest in terms of Olsen's concept of the aesthetic – they deal with significant themes, possess artistic unity, are written in an appropriate style – but are not considered part of the literary canon because they are seen as merely reproducing a past literary form, even if it could be argued that they improve on some of the earliest examples of that form. Thus a tragedy written by a modern playwright in the manner of the Jacobean dramatists is almost certain not to be included in the literary canon in spite of any aesthetic features in Olsen's sense that it may possess. Of course, if that playwright was able to convince the literary community that the tragedy was by Shakespeare it would almost certainly become part of the literary canon, irrespective of aesthetic considerations.

Olsen is right to insist upon the centrality of aesthetics to the concept of literature, but other factors also play a role in determining which texts become part of the literary canon. In claiming that only aesthetic considerations are relevant Olsen comes close to defining literature in immanent terms: 'To understand a literary work as a literary work is thus to understand how its properties (the identification of which are made possible by the institution of literature) contribute to aesthetic value' (ibid.: 24). But in considering literature, aesthetics can no more be kept completely separate from ideology than it can from history. For example, over the past few decades the power of feminism has had a significant influence on the literary canon. Feminist critics have questioned the canonic status of certain texts because of the way they represent women; other texts which undermine female stereotypes have been elevated to canonic status. Before the rise of feminism the representation of women was not an important factor in determining literary merit or value, but now it is. However, it is unlikely, even in the present climate, that a work which is strongly feminist in terms of its ideological position would be accepted into the literary canon if there were wide agreement within the literary community that its aesthetic merits were negligible. Aesthetics, historical considerations and ideology enter into negotiation in the construction of the literary canon.

It seems to me, therefore, that English studies will find it impossible either to discard questions of aesthetics and literary value or to avoid taking account of theoretical, historical or ideological factors. In another contribution to the *London Review of Books* debate on the subject of cultural materialism, Graham Martin points out that those who believe that it is only ideological and political considerations that are responsible for the elevation of Shakespeare and who claim that it has nothing to do with the question of literary value fail to explain why it is Shakespeare's works that 'command the attention of generations of interpreters' (Martin 1990), since the writings of his contemporaries could serve equally well. Yet Alan Sinfield, in responding to Graham Martin, justly points out that Shakespeare's continuing eminence must also be seen in relation to his being 'a powerful cultural token: he is *already* where meaning is produced, and therefore people want to appropriate him' (Sinfield 1990; original emphasis). Sinfield also states, however, that he does 'not rule out factors intrinsic to Shakespeare' (ibid.). What this exchange suggests is that it is impossible to account for Shakespeare or any major canonic writer purely in aesthetic or purely in cultural terms; the two interact inextricably and any attempt to reject one or the other will inevitably fail to convince.

In a recent book, *Exploding English* (1990), Bernard Bergonzi argues that the division in English studies has reached such a pass that those who believe in the literary canon and aesthetic values and those who are committed to literary theory and cultural studies should go their separate ways, with traditional English confining itself to poetry. My contention in this essay is that to imagine that English could be divided in this way is mistaken. To try to wrench the literary and the cultural apart would do serious damage to both and in the long run it would prove impossible for either to maintain a separate existence; each would eventually import aspects of the other. This does not mean to say that there will not be tensions or conflict. Relations between the aesthetic, the cultural, the theoretical will never achieve complete harmony or stability and this will foster debate. But such debate is in my view necessary for English studies.

For nearly two decades English has been, we are told, in a state of crisis, torn apart by its inner contradictions, yet has there ever been a more vital period in literary criticism? This can hardly be a coincidence. It suggests that 'crisis' is healthy for a subject like English. Divisions have come out into the open, creating a recognition of the diverse forces that make up English studies. Only those who are committed to unity for its own sake or who just believe in a quiet life need see this situation negatively. Indeed, since it is impossible to prove that there is any 'right' way to read literary texts, it is inevitable that there will be debate about how they should be read. Rather than avoiding debate by retreating into the 'interpretive community' one happens to favour, such debate should become an intrinsic part of what English studies is about. Thus the ethical and ideological issues raised by how one chooses to read will no longer be avoided. Another way of putting this is that English studies should foreground its dialogical nature and not seek to suppress it. English as a discipline is more threatened by the stifling of that debate, whether that is produced by conservative forces in an institution expelling advocates of theory or cultural studies, or whether it is a consequence of radicals gaining control and demanding that everyone accept and adhere to a particular ideological position.

This debate also has implications beyond English as an academic discipline. The MacCabe affair of the early 1980s briefly made a wider public aware that there was a conflict within English studies when traditionalists at Cambridge succeeded in preventing someone associated with contemporary theory and cultural studies from being appointed to a permanent post. But this conflict was not perceived as having much significance beyond the academic world. Recently, however, the press and other media have again become interested in a conflict which has some relation to the earlier one and which to a large extent centres on the teaching of English in higher education. The emergence of 'political correctness' in American universities, particularly within English departments in which those who reject traditional literary approaches have achieved positions of power, has aroused much adverse comment and has clearly been seen as a threat that could have an impact beyond the academic world. Though I argued above that it would be a negative development if any one tendency achieved a position of power and stifled debate, this does not mean that the issues raised by 'political correctness' are not important, and merely to accuse its supporters of a kind of inverted McCarthyism is no argument against it. These issues will not go away and they need to be debated, with convincing counter-arguments being formulated. But this can happen only if there is a broader awareness of what English as an academic subject involves in the 1990s. A wider public should realise that in an increasing number of institutions it is no longer acceptable to place the greatest emphasis on teaching students to appreciate literary masterpieces; students are also encouraged to engage with aesthetic, cultural and theoretical issues, some of which I have discussed above, and such issues are not merely of academic interest but of wider social significance, as the impact of 'political correctness' on society at large indicates.

There remains the problem of the teaching of English in departments in which there are extremists at both ends of the spectrum. How is teaching in such departments to be organised? Are students not going to be confused? Departments should not try to conceal differences and disagreements from students but on the contrary should, as Gerald Graff has argued, publicise them (Graff 1989). There are bound to be a variety of views among students. They ought to be allowed to change from one teacher to another as a matter of course without any difficulties being created. If, for example, a lecturer committed to a radical cultural studies approach is confronted by a student who says, 'I chose to study English because I'm interested in poetry and I don't therefore want to spend a lot of time reading non-poetic texts which seem to me to have only an indirect relation to poetry as such,' the lecturer should, of course, defend his or her position and seek to persuade the student that he or she is wrong. But if the student refuses to be convinced the lecturer should accept the situation with equanimity and say, 'I'll make arrangements for you to transfer to Dr So-and-so's group.' And it goes without saying that this should also operate in reverse. English departments, in other words, should recognise that division need not mean bitter conflict. Both aesthetically based criticism and a cultural studies approach have sufficient in common to enable them to live together, for though the relation between the two will always be a shifting one and therefore unstable, neither can totally eliminate the other.

NOTE

1 See also Antony Easthope's article (1990) 'The question of literary value' *Textual Practice*, 4: 376–89, which argues that literary value can be objectively determined and cannot be dismissed as an ideological construction. Both Belsey and Easthope are contributors to *Re-Reading English*.

BIBLIOGRAPHY

Beardsley, Monroe C. (1958) *Aesthetics: Problems in the Philosophy of Criticism*, New York: Harcourt, Brace.

Belsey, Catherine (1989) 'Towards cultural history: in theory and practice', *Textual Practice* 3: 159–72.

Bergonzi, Bernard (1990) *Exploding English: Criticism, Theory, Culture*, Oxford: Oxford University Press.

Brooks, Cleanth (1944) 'Empson's criticism', *Accent* 4: 208–16.

de Man, Paul (1971) *Blindness and Insight: Essays in the Rhetoric of Contemporary Criticism*, New York: Oxford University Press.

—— (1982) 'The return to philology', *The Times Literary Supplement*, 10 December: 1,355–6.

Eagleton, Terry (1983) *Literary Theory: An Introduction*, Oxford: Basil Blackwell.

—— (1990) *The Ideology of the Aesthetic*, Oxford: Basil Blackwell.

Ford, Boris (1990) 'Bardbiz', letter in *London Review of Books*, 12 July: 4.

Gates, Henry Louis, Jr (1989) 'Authority, (white) power, and the (Black) critic; or, it's all Greek to me', in Ralph Cohen (ed.) *The Future of Literary Theory*, New York and London: Routledge: 324–46.

Graff, Gerald (1989) 'The future of theory in the teaching of literature', in Ralph Cohen (ed.) *The Future of Literary Theory*, New York and London: Routledge: 250–67.

Greenblatt, Stephen (1980) *Renaissance Self-Fashioning: From More to Shakespeare*, Chicago: University of Chicago Press.

Leavis, F.R. (1947) 'The literary discipline and liberal education', *Sewanee Review* 55: 586–609.

Martin, Graham (1990) 'Bardbiz', letter in *London Review of Books*, 28 June: 4.

Miller, J. Hillis (1974) 'Narrative and history', *English Literary History* 41: 455–73.

—— (1975) 'Deconstructing the deconstructers', *Diacritics* 5: 24–31.

—— (1982) *Fiction and Repetition: Seven English Novels*, Oxford: Basil Blackwell.

Olsen, Stein Haugom (1978) *The Structure of Literary Understanding*, Cambridge: Cambridge University Press.

—— (1987) *The End of Literary Theory*, Cambridge: Cambridge University Press.

Sinfield, Alan (1986) '*Macbeth*: History, ideology and intellectuals', *Critical Quarterly* 28 (1–2): 63–77.

—— (1990) 'Bardbiz', letter in *London Review of Books*, 26 July: 4.

Widdowson, Peter (ed.) (1982) *Re-Reading English*, London: Methuen.

10

TEACHING THEORY
Is it good for us?

Richard Bradford

There is a minor yet well-established tradition of using students as test cases for the validity of educational or interpretive theories. I.A. Richards, Norman Holland and Stanley Fish are probably the best known practitioners of this form of academic democracy, and the ability of Fish's students to replicate the stylistic and interpretive acumen of their tutor is a credit to the US university system. In what follows I shall consider the effects of the past three decades of turmoil in Anglo-American literary theory on the experience of undergraduates in Britain and Ireland. It will not be a comprehensive survey; it will be based upon my own experience and accounts from students and teachers in other institutions. And it will not confine itself to the intellectual flaws and benefits of modern literary theory. Its purpose will be to urge my academic peers to pause for a moment and consider what they are doing and who, if anyone, will benefit from their various techniques and allegiances. It will conclude with a proposal for the restructuring of degree programmes that involve 'reading English'.

THE SHOCK OF THE NEW

First-year undergraduates who have taken 'A' level communication studies might well have encountered such concepts and names as semiotics, Ferdinand de Saussure and C.S. Peirce, but for the vast majority of students of English literature, or humanities combined/cultural studies degree courses, the separation of literature, with its various historical, stylistic and generic designations, from a thing called 'critical and interpretive theory' is a mildly disorientating experience. 'A' level

English or its Scottish and Irish counterparts, the Higher and the Leaving Cert., will have introduced the fresher to what might be called the literary encounter: they will have been encouraged to make and justify judgements on what Lawrence, Donne, Shakespeare or Wordsworth was endeavouring to tell them. What happens next is more a matter of chance than design. The CRAC degree course guide to English and related combinations acknowledges that some institutions offer courses involving structuralism, semiotics, psychoanalysis, linguistics and 'perhaps' feminist critical theory, and advises the prospective student to 'check prospectuses for details'. This might sound wise enough, but there are a number of problems. Approximately one-third of prospectuses actually mention these strange and intimidating terms – understandably perhaps in these days of supply-side academia. A large number of institutions, cutting across what was once the binary divide, and including Cambridge University, Nottingham University, Thames Valley University and Sheffield Hallam University, do make it clear that critical approaches to literature will be dealt with as separate, component courses of the degree, but the average sixth-former is unlikely to inquire further about their allegiances to orthodox 'practical criticism' or to their treatment of literature as part of a network of sign systems. Why? Because, when filling in an UCCA form the merits of spending three years in Bristol as opposed to Glasgow, studying literature as opposed to biology, are more likely to hold the attention than the decoding of a particular department's discrimination between the practical and the theoretical. And without having taken a course in critical theory most sixth-formers are, in any case, unlikely to appreciate the difference.

Postgraduate prospectuses, which give greater details of staff research and teaching interests, and politely 'leaked' reading lists, lead one to conclude that at least 75 per cent of universities, including those newly designated as such, involve their literary studies students in encounters with contemporary critical theory. In many universities, especially the 'ancient' or redbrick type, such courses tend to be optional, whereas in the 'other' types of university (Ulster and Strathclyde for example) and in the majority of ex-polytechnics, critical theory is either designated as a core-compulsory course or implemented as a key disciplinary element of everything from Shakespeare to popular culture. Whatever the permutations of this mixture, the principal problem for the student exists in the distinction between interpretive theory and subject-matter, and here we come upon what can only be described as the guilty secret of English academe.

Statistics supplied by the Council for University English make it clear that something like 65 per cent of all English studies academics are over 40 years of age. Nothing wrong with this of course – experience is to be valued. But what is lacking from the experience of these individuals, and from the majority of the 'new blood' intake, is an encounter, as undergraduates, with the uneasy relation between reading literature and reading theory. Most specialists in a particular field of contemporary literary theory will have achieved their academic standing in two stages. Most will have studied English as undergraduates in universities where far more emphasis is, or would have been, given to the established canon of texts and their position in literary history. Few, if any, would have had the time, opportunity or encouragement to read the collected writings of Kristeva, Jakobson or Derrida before becoming postgraduates or academics.

What we lack is any real certainty that the demands of contemporary theory can be successfully implemented as a component of an undergraduate degree. The arguments, or to be more accurate our arguments, on this issue are roughly as follows. Premiss: since the early 1960s the academic certainties of 'traditional' literary criticism in Anglo-American higher education have been challenged by techniques, assumptions and perspectives borrowed largely from other disciplines – linguistics, psychoanalysis, philosophy, Marxism, sociology and so on. Thesis: to deny students some access to the changes and conflicts within their discipline would be the equivalent of not mentioning Einstein, artificial intelligence and chaos theory to undergraduate physicists.

It is not, of course, as simple as that. Should we 'rope off' critical theory as a separate course and leave the more traditional curricular designations undisturbed? Or should we attempt to redesign entire degree courses in ways that reflect the challenges of theory to the aesthetic elitism, the bourgeois political affiliations or the patriarchal domination of the traditional canon? It is not even as simple as that. If we choose the former do we admit, by implication, that our under-graduates should participate at only a basic and optional level in the intellectual activities demanded of their most innovative, learned and promotion-hungry tutors, and spend the rest of their time with what Terry Eagleton (in *Literary Theory*) calls 'intuitive criticism', which relies not on 'method' but on 'intelligent sensitivity', assisted by dates and footnotes? If so, we acknowledge that what has taxed the higher authorities of critical writing for three decades is of slight relevance to the undergraduate. The second option is even more problematic, because it would be neither practical nor just to oblige teachers who regard theory as a kind of self-indulgent glass-bead game to change their curriculum and teaching practice in accordance with contemporary fashion. These arguments and alternatives have been widely addressed and even tested, but how does the student feel about all of this? The following brew of opinions, complaints and suppositions is drawn from voluntary and largely informal discussions with students at the University of Ulster and Trinity College, Dublin. I rejected the idea of a questionnaire after rereading Empson's account of God's conversation with Adam: I did not want to be told what they assumed that I, who would be marking their essays, wanted to hear.

CONFLICT

The problem of how to balance the demands and attractions of theory against the more basic imperatives of reading all of Shakespeare and judging his qualities against those of his contemporaries varies according to the point at which theory was first encountered. First-year students readily admit to a mixture of disorientation and excitement. The excitement factor is equally prominent for post-sixth-formers and mature students. The primary attraction is the presentation of 'recommended critics' not just as supports to their own uncertain grasp of the text but as representatives of the history of English studies. Chapter 1 of Eagleton's *Literary Theory* is widely praised, as indeed, for those with the time and energy, are Baldick's *The Social Mission of English Criticism* and Lentriccia's *After the New Criticism*. What they like most of all is the opportunity to situate their doubts about the opinions of teachers and writers in relation to their own status as men, women, Irish, English, working-class, middle-class, rather than guiltily dismissing these as temperamental aberrations. Their enthusiasm is tempered by their problem of not knowing, at this point, a great deal about literature.

Bakhtin's theory of the 'carnivalesque' (neatly summarised by Eagleton, Selden, Forgacs *et al.*) is intriguing, but is not really of much use if they have not read Rabelais, the longer Russian and English novels of the nineteenth century or more than one Shakespeare play. Even more troubling is their gradual awareness that there might be no practical benefits to be derived from their new interests. Having received reading lists and course descriptions for the second year, it seems to them that the courses on Shakespeare, on the seventeenth century and on satire neither demand, nor perhaps tolerate, an in-depth awareness of new historicism, hermeneutics and feminism. They like all of this, of course, but they are also concerned about what class of degree they are likely to receive and how this will affect their prospects in the world beyond the gendered signifier. I tell them that although their forthcoming encounters with the canon might give more prominence to fact, detail and expository talent than they would to the semiotic relativity of response, such skills and enlightened perceptions would in fact add an extra, productive dimension to their essays on Blake and Coleridge as visionaries. They know I am lying.

The third-year undergraduates (taking option courses at Ulster and Trinity) present revised but largely consistent versions of the first-year responses. These near-graduates have read a lot of literature and they now have the opportunity to reassess their earlier assumptions about Shakespeare – perhaps he was really a bourgeois icon – or the Romantics, who did not tell us a great deal about the industrial revolution. But, as a number of them inform me, what is the point? In a couple of months it will all be over. They can present me with erudite and even amusing deconstructions of *Moby Dick* or 'Christabel', but unless they get a first and go on into the peculiar world of research, none of this will be relevant. A number of them have noted connections between the currently fashionable idioms of poststructuralism and postmodernism and the oddities of *The Late Show*, *The Word* and half a dozen advertisements, but they are doubtful that their encounters with critical theory will qualify them for entry to the much desired world of 'the media'. Some, being prospective English graduates, have thought about teaching. But, as they enquire with tolerantly knowing inflections, will their knowledge of Foucault and Lacan be of much use to GCSE strugglers or desperate 'A' level candidates?

I could have pointed out to them that university education in English is not primarily vocational; that it taxes and extends our linguistic and analytic competence. It makes us think more closely about who we are and how and why we respond to the aesthetic and non-aesthetic manifestations of our primary communicative medium. I could indeed have presented myself as the poststructuralist-postmodernist version of Matthew Arnold. It seemed dishonest.

POPULARITY

Without doubt the most popular and productive area of current critical theory is feminism. The reasons for this are quite straightforward. Most students have at some point in their lives encountered the social and political manifestations of feminism. Names such as Millett and Greer appear in the popular press and on television and it is likely that any form of encounter between a man and a woman – in soap operas, on the staircase, in bars, in the novel – will be attended by some kind of acknowledged or internalised awareness of sexual difference as an 'issue'. In Ireland particularly, with its unsettled relations between the judiciary and the church, its uncertain present and even more uncertain future, personal freedom and collective responsibility are moving markedly away from the abstractions of political and religious affiliation towards more immediate conflicts between the patriarchy and 'the rest'. In short, the literary–linguistic programme of feminism has direct links with life beyond the increasingly hermetic world of English studies. The question and the problem is how the academic establishment should respond to this sudden opportunity for relevance.

I recently read an essay by a third-year student, subtitled 'The silent woman in the 17th century'. It began with an impressive tour of the more eminent poststructuralists – Lacan on the letter and the body, Derrida on speech and writing, Kristeva on the fetishism of poetic writing – and proceeded to an examination of Portia in *The Merchant of Venice*, Isabella in *Measure for Measure*, the 'Lady' in Milton's *Comus* and the unnamed, silent addressees of Donne's 'The Flea' and Marvell's 'To His Coy Mistress'. Each of these figures was examined as a victim of the patriarchal government of discourse and linguistic exchange. Portia could speak only as a 'man'; Isabella's heroic attempt to match Angelo's judicial rhetoric was quickly marginalised by the Duke's decision that her body – conveniently substituted by Mariana's – was a far more purposive sign than her language; the Lady refused or was unable to engage with Comus' rhetorical strategies, and Donne's and Marvell's addressees function less as characters and more as deictic or formal features of the texts. It was, to say the least, a challenging piece of work, but equally intriguing was its author's *ex-cathedra* comments on its relationship with her other academic commitments.

She acknowledged that she would not have been able to write the essay without the earlier 'ordinary' courses on Shakespeare, the seventeenth century and Milton. What she didn't like was the positioning of 'in-depth' critical theory as an optional extra: first years could be dragged through a simplified, yet still intimidating, schedule of critical types and operations, but their next encounter with these would be three years later – and only then if they felt confident enough to risk their projected 2:1 on the half-remembered weirdness of Derrida or Lacan. For her, theory, particularly feminist theory, had transformed the arcana of stylistics and aesthetic-cultural contexts into patterns that corresponded with the major issues of life in the 1990s: Portia's 'disguise' was not unlike Mrs Thatcher's; Isabella had a great deal in common with Clare Short; the Lady, like her harassed modern counterparts in the office or the bar, had no linguistic defence against the strategies of her demon – she could only refuse to answer or hope for assistance. The problem, as she saw it, was the timing of all this. Feminist theory was useless without a thorough grounding in conventional literary history, and conventional literary history and interpretation were pointless without an understanding of the theoretical challenges to the function, status and identity of 'literature'. Couldn't these two elements be brought closer together throughout the three years, rather than having theory pigeon-holed as an engaging backwater, like the 'war poets' or 'Comedy'? I delivered the well-rehearsed catalogue of practical problems – academics differed on the value of theory, and even if some kind of working compromise could be agreed, how would the system actually work? Would we spend half a term on who the Romantics were and what they did and the other half on how the Marxists diagnosed Romanticism as bourgeois introversion or why the Romantics were so attractive to the deconstructionists? How would all this be examined? Would the student be obliged to write separate essays on the two elements, thus perpetuating the notion of theory as 'different', or could a new system of academic discourse be devised to reflect the interpenetration of theory and literature? The latter proposition is at the heart of the problem: how could we offer students a cohesive, symbiotic relation between contemporary theory and traditional writing and teaching when this issue still splits the academic profession down the middle? She departed, confirmed in her suspicion that academics would rather interrogate and strangle a question than answer it.

To return to the matter of popularity, reception theory and hermeneutics finish a not-too-close second behind feminism. And, again, they earn this status on condition that they are taught as a supplement to a basic awareness of the divisions and subdivisions of literary history. Gadamer's concept of the historical relativity of interpretation, Barthes' distinction between texts *lisible* and *scriptible*, Iser's model of the 'implied reader' equip students, or so they tell me, to deal more confidently with the monoliths of traditional and modernist technique. More significantly, they provide a productive axis between what might be called the protocols of academic exchange and the subjectivity of reading and evaluating texts. One of the ironies of finding oneself temperamentally and intellectually suited to a literature degree emerges from the ease with which one is able to adapt to the mannerisms and conventions of critical language. In short, a response to a text which, in truth, is a combination of irritation, exasperation and sheer boredom can, with practice, be transformed into a learned and respectful interrogation of its stylistic character, its emotional immediacy and its fundamental purpose. One of the most amusing and informative seminars of my recent experience involved the use of Stanley Fish's 'How to recognize a

RICHARD BRADFORD

poem when you see one' (1980) as the 'set text'. For some time
we tossed around the flaws and benefits of Fish's masterly
thesis on the power of the interpretive community, but the
atmosphere changed when Seamus asked why Fish's students
so closely resembled Pavlov's dogs. 'What do you mean?' I
asked. Seamus was impressed by the level of 'literary competence' that would enable a group of students to promote a
random list of surnames on a blackboard to the cultural status
of a seventeenth-century religious lyric, but he was less
impressed by their apparent unwillingness or inability to ask
their eminent professor why they had been prompted to
explicate 'a piece of meaningless crap'.

As the debate progressed, inhibitions loosened and it was
generally agreed that either Fish was fabricating his students'
readings or, even worse, that the celebrated 'authority' of the
interpretive community was in fact a severe disability. Reader-
response theory, it was argued, was an intriguing and sometimes quite useful means of broadening the critical perspective,
but more significantly it reflected the detachment of 'reading
English' in the academy from what actually happened in the
real world of bookselling, publishing and reviewing. The
problem, for them, was how to reconcile their own aesthetic
judgements with what were the unacknowledged but com-
prehensively accepted 'rules' of academic discourse. Fish's
students, though competent in the practices of naturalisation
and the deployment of a critical metalanguage, remained safely
distant from any causal relation between the way they wrote
and their criteria for judging good or bad literature.

We had an hour left, so I introduced a question to which
television and radio arts programmes regularly return: is Bob
Dylan as good a poet as John Keats? Their response, led again
by Seamus, was that it was a stupid comparison. Both of them
occasionally used rhyme, but beyond that no useful purpose
could be served by ignoring the contextual/stylistic differences
between Romantic poetry and folk/rock music of the 1960s.
This, I suggested, was the re-emergence of the widely discredited notion of cultural elitism. No it wasn't, answered
Seamus. Why didn't anyone ask if Stephen Duck was a better
poet than Alexander Pope? Because everyone knew, and could
demonstrate, that he was not. In Seamus's view the Bob Dylan-
Keats question was the consequence of two twentieth-century

170

developments. A lot more people watched films and television and listened to rock music than read literature. But at the same time the study of literature had become a respectable and very popular academic discipline. Hence academics felt the need to make concessions to 'popular culture' (he had recently looked at a couple of New Accents volumes). Popular culture, with a few minor exceptions, has defied all attempts to turn it into literary 'art', so, feeling guilty and not wishing to offend the tastes of the masses, some academics had started denying that 'high art' has any intrinsic and definitive characteristics. But no one was fooled. He remembered reading, in Eagleton's *Literary Theory*, that Bob Dylan was as significant a topic for study as John Milton; he had then found that Eagleton, as general editor of the Re-Reading Literature series, had decided to author the volume on (who else?) William Shakespeare.

Whether or not we regard Seamus's points as valid is of less importance than the context in which he felt able to make them. His contacts with theory had provided him with targets and ammunition and his three years of reading the canon had supplied the battlefield, but it is clear that he and many other students resent the fact that these two elements of the curriculum should for most of their undergraduate career remain separate – largely as a consequence of the academic profession's inability to settle its own differences.

TEACHING

Unless the participants are members of a particular collective of beliefs and affiliations, sharing a lecture programme on critical theory is a dangerous enterprise. In a traditional, period-based course, two or three academics might give wildly divergent appraisals of the intrinsic value or the ideological significance of the work of Dickens, and students will probably benefit from this multidimensional experience. But ask the same figures to 'explain' structuralism and the end result, for students, will often be disorientation and distress. Why? Because the traditional curriculum has always been, and still is, a crucial means of steadying the divergencies, eccentricities, prejudices and sometimes the sheer incompetence of the lecturer. Opinions and methods of delivery might differ, but if the focal point is a stable core of 'set' poems, novels and plays, students can at least balance what they receive against what they have read. Before addressing a group of first years on the origins of the novel we could ask them to read a couple of novels by Defoe and Fielding, and then be secure in our assumption that our discussion of the influence of the picaresque, or of the difficulties of mediating the density of eighteenth-century English society, or even of the new commercial benefits of printing and publishing, would in some way tie in with their encounter with the texts. But how do we go about establishing a similar set-text/lecture relationship for our explanation of the meaning and origins of structuralism? Ask them to read Saussure's *Cours*, a few carefully selected pieces from Lévi-Strauss, an extract or two from Eco and some of the earlier essays of Barthes? We could, but we might be troubled by how to explain the relation between these texts and the primarily linguistic branches of structuralism – the Russian Formalists or the literary offshoots of Chomskyean linguistics and transformational-generative syntax, for instance? More troubling for our students would be the task of first understanding the language and methodology of these linguists and semioticians, and then identifying the practical use of their arcane and complex formulae in the process of literary interpretation. Reading literature would, even for first years, be a familiar, cumulative process of relating text to genre, function and context; the poems, novels and plays are there, a starting point and focus for their intensive and comparative close readings and their extra-textual excursions. But how do they close the gap between an understanding of the differential nature of the linguistic sign and writing essays on the peculiarities of metaphysical verse technique?

The above is, of course, an unreal hypothesis. My question could be answered by a glance at recommended reading lists and publishers' catalogues. We offer them 'guides' to theory. Patrick Parrinder (see pp. 127–44 above) deals mercilessly with the relative qualities of this new brand of pedagogic tool, but what do students think?

Eagleton's *Literary Theory* (1983) is popular mainly because of its stylistic panache and its ability to impart a mixture of angst and superiority. Its less attractive characteristic is its paradoxical assumption that those in need of an 'introduction' will be familiar with the actual methods and results of the theories that Eagleton so confidently savages. The 'Rise of English' chapter is a convincing and attractive polemical exercise, but very few of its fans will be widely read in the critical work of such proto-Fascists as the New Critics and F.R. Leavis. What we need, my students told me about five years ago, is a text that links theory with practice, and the supply-side economics of academe has provided them with a number of possibilities. The most useful, at the moment, seems to be Raman Selden's *Practising Theory and Reading Literature* (1989). A number of my first-year students have found themselves in confident possession of such critical tools as binary oppositions and Barthes' five codes and have joyfully dissected and interrogated texts that their earlier teachers had advised them to treat with submissive respect.

Durant and Fabb's *Literary Studies in Action* (1990) is at once encouraging and, for some academics, disturbing. It moves easily from questions of what is a poetic line and how does the student feel about his/her gender designation, to economic treatments of transformational linguistics and deconstruction. In short, it is an entire curriculum and pedagogic programme in a single book. It embodies a solution to the problem of how to reconcile the division between 'theory' and 'traditional courses', and its largely successful attempt to involve the student in a comprehensive overview of 'literary studies' is an implicit recognition that few, if any, will encounter anything like this in a single degree programme. We are back to the problem of how the past three decades of internal tension can be implemented as a productive 'mix' for undergraduates. Unlike the other 'introduction to theory' guidebooks, *Literary Studies in Action* does not offer itself as a supplement to the students' experience of personal tutor, seminar, lecture, essay and exam. It effectively incorporates these elements of the academic experience, inviting the reader to move from questions of what literature is and how it works to alternative solutions, background reading, practical exercises and ingenious spatial links which feed the methodological and subjective inference of the first question into a network of related issues and textual encounters. In doing this the book anticipates the need for what has come to be known as 'distance learning', and Durant and Fabb should be commended for their foresight.

A number of universities are, at the time of writing, planning the implementation of modular structures, in which each course is a self-contained twelve-to-fifteen-week unit of teaching and examination. This, it is argued, will enable students to pick and choose the components of their degree programme either by working outside the traditional three-year format of their own institution or by acquiring credits (probably over the summer) from other institutions with similar modular arrangements. Speculation abounds, but no one really knows how this system will operate or what its effects are likely to be. It could allow literature students a much broader choice of courses and in effect grant them some control over the ideological and interdisciplinary shape of their own undergraduate careers. First years who acquire a taste for theory could peruse the curricular programmes of other modularised institutions and, within certain limits, shift the emphasis of their next two years of study towards courses that foreground the process and conditions of interpretation and move away from the dominance of the canon. Hence the problem of sixth-formers being unaware of what they are letting themselves in for until they have already started their courses is solved, and in a broader sense the disciplinary divisions and their manifestations in different departments can be offered as a mouthwatering selection of techniques, affiliations and challenges.

This hypothesis is, of course, nonsense. I put it to my third-year group and I can still hear their laughter. A wonderful idea, they agreed, but who has the time and, more importantly, the money to become a travelling scholar? A more likely scenario would be the two-year degree (soon to be offered carrot-like with conditional grant increases), where a twelve-month academic year would mean either an even more limited selection of courses at their base institution or alternatives determined entirely by the proximity of their summer-school to cheap or free accommodation, usually provided by relatives. Contingency and circumstances would replace selection. One suspects that the comprehensiveness and the 'teach-yourself' method of Durant and Fabb looks forward to the needs of a student literally unattached to a particular department, let alone a tutor.

It is likely, probably inevitable, that the 'universities' - which now include those institutions that were once designated as polytechnics and higher education colleges - will be divided up into a kind of academic Barclays league, with a superdivision (ten or fifteen?) of research institutions at the top, and everyone else programmed and funded to deal primarily with the brisk and economic disposal of knowledge. We might no longer be an aircraft carrier for the USA's nuclear arsenal, but we are rapidly becoming a parochial offshoot of its higher education system. It is unlikely that we, as academics, will be allowed any say in these developments, so what can we do?

The problems are varied and complex. Some, though not all, of us will soon have to deal with summer teaching (some in the new universities already have). Some, depending on the disposition of our vice-chancellor and our grading in the research production game, will have to sign new contracts committing us to teaching or to research-teaching. We will in any event have to teach a lot more undergraduates than our experience and expectations have prepared us for and the possibility of 'distance learning' is being widely debated as a solution. In a broader context, the reputation and status of the humanities 'don' have sunk rapidly in popular and probably in donnish perceptions: what do we actually contribute to the perennial battle against economic slumps, or to the 'appalling' intellectual and behavioural condition of the population at large?

Compared with these conditions and imperatives, the internal division between 'theory' and 'tradition' in literary studies seems to slip easily into the background. But, in a paradoxical way, the new academic landscape could be just what is needed to make us actually do something about closing the gap between the undergraduate experience and the internalised debate about the purpose and future of literary criticism as an academic discipline. In what follows I shall offer a hypothesis and a series of proposals. I write as a member of a lower division of the Barclays league, but my propositions are addressed also to those whose academic futures might seem to be a lot more comfortable.

THE STUDENT OF THE 1990s

All prospective undergraduates of the 1990s will face a number of related problems and we can reduce these to three principal categories: finance; the difficulties of working in an environment that will be, to put it mildly, overcrowded; and their prospects after earning a BA. Some will, of course, benefit from the resources and the generosity of their families, but let us base this hypothesis on the person facing the most uninviting circumstances. This applicant left school at the age of 16, and after about eight years of paid if uninspiring work she considers re-entering the education system as a mature student. She might well have a child, and she might not be able, or want, to depend upon the financial and domestic assistance of a family or partner. What would prompt such an individual to enroll for a degree course in literary studies? In practical terms, not much, but in my own experience of mature students who fit this or something like this profile, the academic attractions of learning are at least as important as its projected financial or vocational benefits. Such a person might well be drawn to the 'fast-track' two-year degree or to a credit accumulation system that would allow her or him to shape academic work around more demanding imperatives of family and finance. From the academic's perspective such students offer a number of challenges. Their encounters with the world outside the education system will have given them the experience, if not the methodology, to question the implied but rarely stated assumptions about the 'value' of literary studies. If you've had a child and experienced the attendant social, ethical and practical problems, the distinction between Mary Shelley's *Frankenstein* and Percy Bysshe's ruminations on existential crisis will become more keenly edged than they would be for the academic who is actually paid for raising such issues, or for the 17 or 18 year-old post-sixth-former for whom the processing of 'Romanticism' is just the next task in an academic schedule still largely detached from her or his encounters with the real world. In an important sense this world-wise student is the test case for the future of literary studies. So how should we go about meeting the challenge?

THESIS–ANTITHESIS : A METHOD OF TEACHING

First of all consider the practical problems of planning a modular course covering a single element of 'literary studies'. Providing an accessible and relevant unit on, say, Romanticism or seventeenth-century literature for a student whose degree programme is based on the interdisciplinary salad of humanities combined or cultural studies will be a familiar task to many ex-polytechnic and some (particularly the 'Open') university teachers, but the difficulties will increase with students who might have just returned after a one- or two-year break or whose immediate experience of the demands and parameters of reading English has been acquired somewhere else. It seems to me that the traditional designation by historical period should be retained in a large number of courses, while allowing for such ahistorical, conceptual courses as women writers or post-colonial literature. What should change is the way in which we integrate the canon, the 'set texts' of the course, with matters such as history, ideology and gender representation, and here the complaints of the third-year essayist of 'Silent women of the 17th century' should be taken into account. The course will be called 'Shakespeare', but this will be its principal concession to traditionalism.

Assume that the module/semester lasts twelve to fourteen weeks, with ten weeks of teaching. Twenty lectures of not more than forty minutes will be given, leaving fifteen or twenty minutes for questions and student–teacher exchanges (intimate tutorials will probably be a cherished memory). Each week the first lecture will cover a specific interpretive issue or an individual Shakespeare text and the second will extend and interrogate this text–reader model. On Tuesday we will consider *Measure for Measure*; its status as a 'problem play', its shifts between blank verse and prose, its function as a commentary on governing the city-state of London in 1604, its ability to reflect the ascribed roles of men and women in seventeenth-century English society (ten minutes per issue). On Friday this same quartet of textual functions will be re-examined. Why are the 'problem plays' more problematic than the rest? Does this tell us something about the relation between 'literary' discourse (unsituated, unrelated to the purposive candour and objectives of non-literary discourse)? What does the shift between poetic and non-poetic discourse actually involve? Are the speaking subjects (introduce Benveniste) of the blank-verse sequences functions and determinants of language, unlike the apparently unconstrained users of prose? And what does this tell us about the relation between aesthetics and the social hierarchy? (Bakhtin's notion of the carnivalesque might become relevant at this point.) What does Shakespeare's image of a city-state in moral and social decay tell us about the ability, or inability, of literature to reflect or mediate conditions of social and political turmoil? Here we could introduce the concept of Marxist and non-Marxist perceptions of the literary function. Finally, how do we judge the relation between Isabella, Mariana, Juliet, Mistress Overdone and Angelo, the Duke, Claudio and Lucio? Are the former effectively governed by the thematic and, it is implied, social imperatives of the text? What does this tell us about the representation of women in sixteenth- and seventeenth-century literature, and how does this relate to feminist perceptions of the patriarchal conditons of the sixteenth- to twentieth-century canon? (An entire tradition of interpretive issues can here be introduced: the maleness of metaphysical lyric, Sandra Gilbert on Milton, Ellen Moers on Mary Shelley, and so on.) Similar textual–interpretive/contextual interactions can be foregrounded, on Tuesdays and Fridays, with: *Hamlet* – psychoanalysis and feminism; *Henry V* – literature and propaganda; *The Tempest* – 'baring the device', literature as a self-referential discourse; *Titus Andronicus* – the popular appeal of the sordid and violent, looking forward to Webster as the seventeenth-century anticipation of the video nasty; the 'Sonnets' – poetry as an enclosed textual world.

My microcosmic concentration of the conflicts of literary studies into a weekly alternation between text and theory, thesis and antithesis, might sound simplistic and over-optimistic, but as a practical means of reconciling the distinctions between academic affiliations, research interests and the demands of teaching, it does, I believe, deserve further consideration. Its success would depend upon the weekly designation of specific issues or texts. For students this would maintain the anchoring function of the set text and would supplement this with a live performance of their very often confusing encounters with 'background reading'. It would probably take them several months to begin to appreciate the vast disciplinary distinctions between Empson and Belsey on Milton, or Kermode and Eagleton on Shakespeare, but to have two lecturers who address exactly the same issues from the feminist and non-feminist perspectives would allow them first to examine their individual responses to the problems of interpretation and then to enter the jungle of critical reading with far more confidence.

Consider, for example, the problematic relation between literary studies and linguistics. Courses on 'language' or 'stylistics' can often present themselves as marginal to the demands and preconditions of a canon-based literature degree. But what if a lecturer whose interests lay in the sociopolitical relevance of Wordsworth and Coleridge, their uneasy, innovative relation with the eighteenth century and their biographical profiles, were to give a lecture on three designated poems, and a specialist in Jakobsonian and Formalist method, transformational and generative grammar and literature as an element of social discourse were to consider the same three texts? The benefits of a text-based lecture schedule would be preserved, but the division between literary study and linguistics as separate academic designations and consequently separate courses would be transformed into purposive integration.

A course on feminism or women in literature could maintain a similar emphasis on individual texts as the focus for literary and non-literary divisions. A Miltonist could arrive on Tuesday to consider the cultural, stylistic, moral and historical characteristics of *Paradise Lost*, to be followed on Friday by lecturer who would use this text as a starting point for a much broader examination of the representation of the female stereotype and the function of sexual difference as a structural and thematic element of the canon. The established canon is important because, like the other intellectual, political, linguistic or architectural constituents of our inheritance, it cannot be made to disappear. A lecture sequence based upon alternation between attitudes and suppositions would allow students to balance and judge the relation between tradition and the more recent diversities of theory. The problem of examining such a degree programme would have to be debated by its teachers, but these debates would be grounded upon the knowledge that any question on a particular text can never remain immune from the student's experience of the close, if unsettled, relationship between literature and theory.

The problems and benefits of such an inter-institution programme are mutually productive. Let us return to the

'Shakespeare' course. For students whose encounters with literature and the broader contextual format of the canon are more limited than those of the three-year single honours English undergraduate, such a course would provide an axis between the traditional notion of the English Renaissance and the more demanding framework of interpretation and the canon. Moreover, theory can be offered not as an alternative to traditional literary studies but as a pattern of political and analytical codes that cannot be isolated from literary studies, and which indeed is often incited and challenged by literature. The course would satisfy the modular criterion of self-containment (sixteenth- and seventeenth-century literature), while offering students paths towards the study of other literary periods and access to interpretive programmes that will allow them to consider how concepts such as periodisation and the canon came into existence and how the study of literature is, or is not, valuable in their encounters with more immediate issues such as the history and perpetuation of the patriarchy and the relation between language and politics. Our test-case mature student would realise her objective of knowing more about literature, but, more significantly, she would graduate as someone who is willing and able to engage with the uneasy relation between what we are and how our primary communicative medium plays an important part in our perceptions of our status as male–female, privileged–unprivileged, cultured–uncultured. I might sound naive and over-optimistic, but we must live in hope.

How would such a programme of modules be implemented by an academic discipline still divided between theorists and traditionalists? In my experience the presentation of thesis and antithesis is attractive to students, but less so when these divisions manifest themselves as separate courses. It would not be beyond the practical demands of teaching to ask the traditionalist Shakespearean to give the first paper on Shakespeare, to be followed by the theorist. Clearly, the specificity of topics and issues would have to be agreed - or perhaps argued over - by the participants. But such immediate, practical demands and encounters would shift the disciplinary division away from the letters pages of the *Times Literary Supplement* towards the more productive and fruitful forum of the academic workplace.

TO CLOSE

The most divisive and widely misinterpreted point of division between theorists and anti-theorists is the question of why and consequently how we should teach literature in higher education. The familiar and battered targets for the iconoclasts are Arnold, Leavis and the New Critics, and most of us are now convinced that the privileged, hermetic world of literary studies as something that inculcates moral, linguistic and social order is an illusion. But for the iconophiles the alternatives are even more distressing: the pollution of the literary hierarchy with 'film' or media studies; the isolation of literary criticism as a weird and self-referential discourse that the average reader would neither be able nor wish to understand (see Kermode's much referred-to article on 'The decline and fall of the readable literary critic', *Guardian*, 10 October 1991). This division is, in my experience, an internalised academic phenomenon. If we can devise a method of offering these conflicts as a productive and accessible forum for undergraduates, we will also provide ourselves with that long sought-after objective, an audience, and a link between the academic and non-academic worlds. Most students, even those whose academic affiliations are influenced by the semiotics and sociology of media studies, respect the 'otherness' of literature. But what they demand is a degree course that allows them to follow paths and links between the acknowledged peculiarities and self-determined isolation of literature and the non-literary means by which twentieth-century human beings entertain themselves, behave and think. We, as a collective of individuals whose prejudices and affiliations are widely diverse, are perfectly equipped to provide them with such a programme. We should not stop arguing among ourselves, but we should offer these same arguments as an interactive and purposive component of our degree structure.

BIBLIOGRAPHY

Baldick, Christopher (1983) *The Social Mission of English Criticism 1848–1932*, Oxford: Clarendon Press.
Durant, Alan and Fabb, Nigel (1990) *Literary Studies in Action*, London: Routledge.

Eagleton, Terry (1983) *Literary Theory: An Introduction*, Oxford: Basil Blackwell.

Fish, Stanley (1980) 'How to recognize a poem when you see one', in *Is There a Text in This Class?*, Cambridge, Mass.: Harvard University Press.

Forgacs, David (1982) 'Marxist literary theories', in Anne Jefferson and David Robey (eds) *Modern Literary Theory: A Comparative Introduction*, London: Batsford.

Jefferson, Anne, and Robey, David (eds) (1982) *Modern Literary Theory: A Comparative Introduction*, London: Batsford.

Lentriccia, Frank (1980) *After the New Criticism*, Chicago: Chicago University Press.

Selden, Raman (1989) *Practising Theory and Reading Literature: An Introduction*, London: Harvester Wheatsheaf.

INDEX